Sport, economy and society
in Britain, 1750–1914

New Studies in Economic and Social History

Edited for the Economic History Society by
Michael Sanderson
University of East Anglia, Norwich

This series, specially commissioned by the Economic History Society, provides a guide to the current interpretations of the key themes of economic and social history in which advances have recently been made or in which there has been significant debate.

In recent times economic and social history has been one of the most flourishing areas of historical study. This has mirrored the increasing relevance of the economic and social sciences both in a student's choice of career and in forming a society at large more aware of the importance of these issues in their everyday lives. Moreover specialist interests in business, agricultural and welfare history, for example, have themselves burgeoned and there has been an increased interest in the economic development of the wider world. Stimulating as these scholarly developments have been for the specialist, the rapid advance of the subject and the quantity of new publications make it difficult for the reader to gain an overview of particular topics, let alone the whole field.

New Studies in Economic and Social History is intended for students and their teachers. It is designed to introduce them to fresh topics and to enable them to keep abreast of recent writing and debates. All the books in the series are written by a recognised authority in the subject, and the arguments and issues are set out in a critical but unpartisan fashion. The aim of the series is to survey the current state of scholarship, rather than to provide a set of pre-packaged conclusions.

The series has been edited since its inception in 1968 by Professors M. W. Flinn, T. C. Smout and L. A. Clarkson, and is currently edited by Dr Michael Sanderson. From 1968 it was published by Macmillan as *Studies in Economic History*, and after 1974 as *Studies in Economic and Social History*. From 1995 *New Studies in Economic and Social History* is being published on behalf of the Economic History Society by Cambridge University Press. This new series includes some of the titles previously published by Macmillan as well as new titles, and reflects the ongoing development throughout the world of this rich seam of history.

For a full list of titles in print, please see the end of the book.

Sport, economy and society in Britain 1750–1914

Prepared for the Economic History Society by

Neil Tranter
University of Stirling

CAMBRIDGE
UNIVERSITY PRESS

PUBLISHED BY THE PRESS SYNDICATE OF THE UNIVERSITY OF CAMBRIDGE
The Pitt Building, Trumpington Street, Cambridge CB2 1RP, United
Kingdom

CAMBRIDGE UNIVERSITY PRESS
The Edinburgh Building, Cambridge CB2 1RU, United Kingdom
40 West 20th Street, New York, NY 10011-4211, USA
10 Stamford Road, Oakleigh, Melbourne 3166, Australia

First published 1998

Printed in Great Britain at the University Press, Cambridge

Typeset in 10/12½ pt Plantin

A catalogue record for this book is available from the British Library

Library of Congress Cataloguing in publication data

Tranter, Neil.
  Sport, economy and society in Britain, 1750–1914/prepared
  for the Economic History Society by Neil Tranter.
     p.   cm. – (New studies in economic and social history)
  Includes bibliographical references and index.
  ISBN 0 521 57217 7 (hc). – ISBN 0 521 57655 5 (pb)
  1. Sports – Social aspects – Great Britain – History – 18th century.
  2. Sports – Economic aspects – Great Britain – History – 18th century.
  3. Sports – Social aspects – Great Britain – History – 19th century.
  4. Sports – Economic aspects – Great Britain – History – 19th century.
  5. Sports – Social aspects – Great Britain – History – 20th century.
  6. Sports – Economic aspects – Great Britain – History – 20th century.
  I. Economic History Society. II. Title. III. Series.
  GV706.5.T73 1998
  306.4' 83' 0941 – dc21
  97–23648 CIP

ISBN 0 521 57217 7 hardback
ISBN 0 521 57655 5 paperback

Contents

1
Introduction

From the dawn of human civilisation, it seems, the need for some form of sporting physical recreation has been almost as imperative to human beings as the need to procreate, work and eat. In practice, of course, the extent to which this need was satisfied varied greatly from time to time and place to place. In some pre-industrial societies opportunities for indulging in sport were often severely circumscribed by adverse demographic, economic or political circumstances. In others, like that of mid-eighteenth century Britain, environmental circumstances were more favourable and levels of participation in sport accordingly much higher. Yet, thriving though it was, the sporting culture of the early Georgian age was in many fundamental respects very different from that which had emerged by 1914. Compared with its Edwardian successor, the sporting world of 1750 was restricted in the number of sports it offered and the percentage of the population it regularly attracted. It was also localised in its geographic range, irregular in its availability and timing and largely devoid of institutional structures and commonly accepted written rules – and disturbingly violent. Admittedly, none of these characteristics were entirely absent from the sporting culture of the Edwardian period. They were, however, no longer sport's predominant features. Excessively violent sports had either almost completely disappeared or, as illustrated by the transition from bare-knuckle prize-fighting to gloved boxing under Marquis of Queensberry rules, been transformed into far less brutal recreations. The range of sports available and the numbers of people playing and watching them had markedly increased. Sport had become extensively institutionalised, codified and commercialised and had spread beyond a purely local or regional arena into national and even international competition.

Above all, perhaps, the reasons for participating had changed. By 1914 it was no longer considered sufficient to take part in sporting pastimes chiefly, let alone solely, for the pleasure they brought. As never before, the sporting proselytisers of late Victorian and Edwardian Britain had endowed physical recreation with a battery of serious purposes which in combination had gone far towards transforming it from a simple source of fun and relaxation to a device thought essential for the continued success of Anglo-Saxon civilisation.

What follows is an attempt to summarise the efforts of historians and historical sociologists to unravel the detailed chronology and nature of this 'revolution' in sporting culture, the forces which propelled it, and the effects it had on the wider evolution of cultural, social and economic life. Particular attention will be paid to the questions most frequently treated in the current literature. Did the extent of popular sport increase or decrease during the initial surge of urban industrialisation in the late eighteenth and early nineteenth centuries (chapter 2)? When, precisely, did the new culture of sport first effectively emerge and what were its principal features and the mechanisms responsible for its spread (chapter 3)? What were its underlying causes and the objectives of its supporters, and how far were these objectives attained (chapters 4 and 5)? To what extent did females participate in the sporting 'revolution' and why was their participation so limited (chapter 6)?

As the final chapter will show, a good deal more research, particularly of an empirical kind, will be required before our understanding of one of the most impressive, if until recently neglected, innovations of Victorian and Edwardian Britain can be considered satisfactory. But at least the basis for a fuller understanding has already been laid. This synopsis is dedicated to the scholars who have helped prepare this foundation. To those whose contributions I have drawn upon but, because of constraints of space, been unable to acknowledge directly I apologise unreservedly.

2

Growth or decline? The initial impact of urban industrialisation

Of the many controversial issues that have emerged from the recent burgeoning of academic interest in the history of sport in Britain, one of the most enduring has concerned the effect of economic and demographic change on the extent of sporting activity among the working classes in the period between the late eighteenth and mid-nineteenth centuries. Writing at a time when it was fashionable to regard this period as one of revolutionary economic and demographic development, the earliest academic historians of sport were generally agreed that the initial impact of urban industrialisation and population growth on popular sport was detrimental. Most forcibly expressed by Robert Malcolmson, the belief that a once thriving mass sporting culture began to decline during the later decades of the eighteenth century and had largely disappeared by the onset of the Victorian era was shared by all (Malcolmson, 1973: 118–57; Dunning, 1975: 112; Walvin, 1978: 2–3; Dunning and Sheard, 1979: 40–1).

Fundamental to this decline, it was argued, was a multiplicity of factors which, on the one hand, diminished the willingness and ability of working-class people themselves to participate in sport and, on the other, eroded that active, or at least passive, support of the social elite which was assumed to be crucial to the existence of a buoyant mass sporting culture. For some working-class men, imbued with a growing desire for respectability and increasingly disenchanted by their dependence on the paternalism of their social superiors, the decision to abandon customary sporting practices was seen to have been largely self-determined. For most, however, it was explained as an unwanted but unavoidable consequence of what was assumed to be a rapidly changing environment. As small, personal and tightly knit rural communities increasingly gave way to larger, more impersonal and more mobile urban communities, as agriculture became increasingly commercialised and as the balance of employment shifted from agriculture to manufacturing and from domestic handicraft industries to factories, so forces emerged that were inimical to the survival of many established sporting customs.

One of these, we are told, was a reduction in the amount of time available for leisure caused by the requirement of factory industry and commercialised agriculture for longer and more regular hours of work from their employees. A second was urbanisation and the enclosure of waste and common land which reduced the amount of space available for play. A third, feeding on the values of the Enlightenment and Evangelical and Methodist hostility to wordly pleasures generally and Sabbath recreations in particular, was the spread of more sensitive, humanitarian attitudes which condemned cruel and violent sports as creators of brutal, immoral and criminal men and thus as impediments to the progress of civilisation. Another was the establishment of more effective systems of policing and the growing use made of these by local authorities anxious to stamp out those popular sporting pastimes considered inappropriate to the needs of large urban communities where the interests of public order, property security and profit maximisation were more urgent than in the smaller, essentially rural communities of earlier times.

To these explanations for the presumed decline in plebeian sport was added yet another, the widespread withdrawal of aristocratic and gentry patronage. Exacerbated by events in France, it was claimed, the feelings of insecurity provoked among the landed elites by the increasing size and influence of the urban bourgeoisie forced the landowning aristocracy and gentry back into their own largely exclusive social world, thereby depriving the sports of the masses of the patronage on which they had hitherto so heavily relied. In the absence of extensive bourgeois support for working-class sporting recreations, the inevitable outcome was an almost complete vacuum in popular sport. By the second quarter of the nineteenth century a thriving sporting culture persisted only

among the landed elites whose often no less cruel sports were pro-
tected from criticism by the fact that they were practised on private
ground by men who were assumed too civilised to be corrupted by
the potentially brutalising influence of the sports they pursued
(Malcolmson, 1973: 89–117, 158–71; Dunning, 1975: 112;
Walvin, 1978: 3–11; Dunning and Sheard, 1979: 41–4; Delves,
1981: 105–8, 113, 115).

Almost from its inception this interpretation of the initial
impact of urban industrialisation on working-class sport was subject to criticism. That many popular sports came under increasing
attack in the late eighteenth and early nineteenth centuries has
never been disputed. What has been disputed is the effectiveness of
this attack. Recent, more detailed analysis of such admittedly fragmentary evidence as exists has shown that the only working-class
sports for which there is indisputable proof of decline were those
blood sports involving animals; and even these, it is now believed,
survived more extensively than was once assumed (Cunningham:
1980, 22–4). In London the sports of badger-baiting and cockfighting persisted throughout the first half of the nineteenth century. Cockfighting continued in some parts of Scotland until at
least the 1850s and, though less prevalent than before the 1830s,
was still common in mining districts of south Northumberland as
late as the 1870s (Metcalfe, 1982: 475; Tranter, 1987a: 29). Dog-
fighting, hare and rabbit coursing and ratting were other animal
blood sports which, at least in some areas and among some sections of the working-class population, had by no means wholly disappeared by the middle years of the nineteenth century (Holt,
1989: 57–63).

In the case of most other working-class sporting recreations the
weight of such evidence as we have suggests growth or, at worst,
stability rather than persistent, pronounced decline. Throughout
the first half of the nineteenth century sculling and rowing continued to attract working-class participants and vast numbers of
working-class spectators to its principal locations on the Thames,
the Tyne, the south coast and in Cornwall and north-west England. Between 1835 and 1851 around 5,000 sculling contests are
known to have taken place on the Thames alone (Wigglesworth,
1986: 147–51; Halladay, 1987: 40; Holt, 1989: 22–3). Prize-
fighting, which originated in the seventeenth century, grew in

popularity from the 1790s and showed no sign of declining until the 1840s, or even later (Holt, 1989: 20–1; Shipley, 1989: 78–9). The number of curling clubs in Scotland increased rapidly from the 1770s and by 1848 the Grand Caledonian Curling Club, the sport's controlling body, boasted 8,000 members and 187 affiliated clubs, nearly five times the number that had existed at the beginning of the century. Shinty continued to flourish in lowland Scotland until the 1840s, though only in Edinburgh and Glasgow did its popularity actually increase. As attested by the construction of the first purpose-built running tracks and the enormous crowds attracted to watch star performers like Captain Barclay, the popularity of pedestrianism (professional athletics) soared between the 1750s and 1860s, by which time it was probably the most extensive working-class sporting interest. Knurr and spell, potshare, or long bowling, quoiting and wrestling were among many other working-class sports which either grew in appeal or, at worst, survived on a healthy regional basis throughout the first half of the nineteenth century and sometimes beyond (Cunningham, 1980: 27; Brailsford: 1982, 41, 44, 47; Holt, 1989: 57–73; Tranter, 1990a). Horseracing remained popular in many localities, cricket continued to expand and even folk forms of football may have persisted outside the confines of the elite private schools more extensively than it was once customary to suppose (Vamplew, 1976: 17–28; 1989: 215–16; Holt, 1988: 70–2; Metcalfe, 1988: 270; Tranter, 1990b: 192–3; Murray, 1994: 10–11; Sandiford, 1994: 19–31).

By focusing too narrowly on the most brutal and turbulent working-class sports with the greatest potential for fostering moral decay and social disturbance the academic pioneers of sport history tended to overlook the very different experience of other working-class sports for which clear evidence of decline is either entirely lacking or less than conclusive. Too readily they assumed that the erosion of animal blood sports like cockfighting, throwing at cocks, bear and badger baiting and bullrunning, and the efforts of the authorities to stamp out particularly violent and unruly sports like football and prize-fighting, were representative of what happened to popular sport as a whole. Recent work, more aware of the resilience of even those traditional sports which did decline, and incorporating a wider range of sports which attracted less opprobrium and showed little or no sign of significant decline, is less pessimistic and less inclined to accept the notion of a vacuum in popular sport in the second quarter of the nineteenth century (Golby and Purdue, 1984: 63–83, 89–90; Tranter, 1987a; Speak, 1988: 61; Vamplew, 1988a: 10; 1988b: 40; Holt, 1989: 57–73). On the whole, this latter interpretation sits more comfortably not only with what we now know about the evolution of sport itself but also with current consensus on the general character of the economic and social changes which occurred between the late eighteenth and mid-nineteenth centuries.

As Hugh Cunningham was the first to stress, the twin processes of accelerating rates of population growth and rapid urbanisation created an environment that was as likely to encourage as discourage popular sport. At a time when there is no reason to assume that the working-class desire for recreation was any less acute than it had previously been, the emergence of large urban communities, for most of whose inhabitants real incomes remained stable in the first quarter of the century and rose in the second quarter, opened up new commercial opportunities for the enterprising to exploit. To judge from the renewed vitality of sports like prize-fighting and quoiting and the growing popularity of circuses and travelling menageries, pantomimes, singing salons and theatres, the entre-preneurial response to these opportunities was dynamic (Bailey, 1978: 9–34; Cunningham, 1980: 36–51). Evidence on the geo-graphic distribution of sporting activity in late eighteenth and mid-nineteenth-century Scotland, based on contemporary statements in the Old and New Statistical Accounts, provides further confir-mation of Cunningham's thesis. Both in the 1790s and 1830s/1840s outdoor sports were more prevalent in lowland regions of Scotland, where urbanisation and rates of population growth were greatest, than in Highland and Island regions, where urbanisation was negligible and the population more scattered and growing more slowly (Tranter, 1987a: 26–7, 30). In Scotland, at least, the positive effects of population growth and urbanisation on the size of the market for sporting recreations clearly outweighed the negative effects that may have stemmed from shortages of space and the requirements of public order and property security.

There is a current preference among economic historians for seeing the process of economic development in late eighteenth- and early nineteenth-century Britain as more gradual and piecemeal and less revolutionary and pervasive than it was once thought to be. Accordingly, the belief of earlier historians of sport that popular sporting traditions were undermined by the demands of employers for longer and more regular hours of work no longer seems quite so convincing. As late as 1851 only a small minority of the male labour force was employed in those few factory and mining enterprises where working hours are known to have increased. For the large majority of workers, in manufacturing and mining no less than in agriculture and the services, the organisational and technological nature of employment changed little before the second half of the nineteenth, and there was consequently no serious threat to recreational time. Hence, in London, where manufacturing continued to be dominated by small craft industries, much of the old artisan culture of leisure survived. In rural Oxfordshire the traditional festivities associated with the Whitsun holiday remained largely intact until at least the late 1830s. In Scotland, despite the growing scale and sophistication of agricultural and industrial production, sport was more not less common in the 1830s/1840s than in the 1790s (Tranter, 1987a: 30). Even in Lancashire, where factory methods of production were most prevalent, the traditional wakes holidays and the recreations bound up with them did not disappear until much later in the century. Moreover, instances like the football match played in 1835 between workers from the Blairdrummond estates and the Deanston cotton mills, which the latter were reported to have won partly because 'while the mossmen have had no practice of late, the Deanston boys omit few opportunities of trying their agility in this manly game', indicate that even factory workers were not always precluded from regular participation in sport (Tranter, 1990b: 193).

There are several reasons for questioning the validity of the notion that working-class sports were fatally damaged by the withdrawal of aristocratic and gentry patronage. First, as yet we have far too little quantitative empirical evidence to permit a secure generalisation about overall trends in the extent of such patronage. It is undoubtedly the case that by the early nineteenth century the aristocracy and gentry were steadily reducing their support of those animal blood sports most closely associated with the working classes. On the other hand, motivated by paternalist traditions which regarded patronage as one of the responsibilities of privilege and the patronising of plebeian sport as a means of ensuring social harmony, they continued to support a wide range of other sports in which there was extensive working-class involvement – boatracing, cricket, curling, horseracing, quoiting and even some of the more violent recreations like football and pugilism (Holt, 1989: 21–6; Sandiford, 1994: 21). The problem is that in the present state of knowledge we cannot tell whether their support of these latter sports grew more or less rapidly than the decline which occurred in their support of the former. Until this problem is resolved aggregate levels of aristocratic and gentry patronage will remain unclear.

Secondly, even if a general decline in the flow of patronage from the landed elites is confirmed by future research, it is possible that some, or perhaps all, of the resulting void was filled by patrons from other social groups. The significance of one alternative source of support for working-class sport – that supplied by publicans – has already been amply documented for sports such as boatracing, cricket and pedestrianism and its influence was probably no less vital for others such as prize-fighting, quoiting and skittles. Recent demonstrations of a flourishing sports culture in eighteenth- and early nineteenth-century English and Scottish elite schools and universities, together with examples like the John Hope Football Club of Edinburgh, which suggest that this was sometimes continued into adulthood, also raise the possibility that the urban professional and business elites of early nineteenth-century Britain were neither so hostile to nor so devoid of sporting recreations as it has been customary for most historians to suppose (Anderson, 1987; Chandler, 1988a and 1988b; Tranter, 1993). To date, it is true, there is no evidence to suggest that this interest in sport among the urban bourgeoisie was carried over into an active patronage of working-class sport. But this may be because historians have not yet looked hard enough to find it. Conceivably, Robert Owen's insistence on the inclusion of physical education, games and drill in the curriculum of his school at New Lanark is indicative of a wider sympathy for working-class sport among the urban middle classes that is still waiting to be uncovered.

Thirdly, as Reid (1988) and Flett (1989) note, even in cases like the disappearance of mass football matches from the streets of towns such as Derby, Louth and Worcester, where the withdrawal of traditional sources of patronage was clearly a contributing factor, it was probably one of the least important of a variety of influences which between them determined the survival or demise of individual sports. For urban communities in particular, to assume that working-class sport as a whole was so dependent on the sponsorship of the landed elites that it could not survive without it is to oversimplify the causes of a complex phenomenon. This assumption also both overstates the influence of the aristocracy and gentry and understates the capacity of working-class culture to determine its own character and evolution. That some plebeian sports decreased in popularity in the course of the late eighteenth and early nineteenth centuries was chiefly the result of other factors than the withdrawal of landed elite support.

It was the most brutal and disruptive pastimes like football and prize-fighting and the animal blood sports of the working classes that were most frequently condemned and most prone to decline. This has convinced more recent historians of sport that of all the forces hostile to the survival of traditional working-class sporting recreations the most influential was the pursuit of higher standards of private and public behaviour triggered by a wider acceptance of Enlightenment, Evangelical and Methodist values repugnant to unnecessary violence and cruelty. In their explanations for the increasing opposition of the social elites to street football and the animal blood sports of the masses, sport historians nowadays are more inclined to emphasise the desire for respectability than the concerns of property owners and businessmen for public order and workforce discipline. Lacking convincing proof of radical, wholesale changes in hours and conditions of work, the urge for respectability also helps us to understand why at least some of the more skilled members of working-class society willingly supported authorities' attempts to rid society of its most brutal and potentially most morally degrading pastimes. They, too, condemned the immorality and turbulence associated with some of the old sports and shared the view that, in a more enlightened and humanitarian age, these should yield to more acceptable and uplifting recreations. The reformation in popular manners, and the hostility to some established sporting customs which it helped to generate, was the result of pressure from below as well as from above (Delves, 1981: 106; Reid, 1988; Flett, 1989; Bailey, 1989: 114–15; Holt, 1989: 38–43).

At the same time the impact of a growing desire for respectability on the extent of working-class sport was bound to be limited. For one thing, most of the sports practised by the labouring classes were largely immune from criticism either because, like cricket or horseracing, they were shared with the elites or because, like quoiting or rowing, they appeared to offer no serious threat to a respectable lifestyle. For another, while the artisans and skilled workers who made up the labour aristocracy were often as committed to the pursuit of respectability as their middle-class superiors, bourgeois notions of respectability were far less evident among the unskilled and semi-skilled, who comprised the bulk of the labouring population. The protracted nature of the struggle to rid towns like Derby of street football and the long persistence of animal blood sports in places like London and the mining communities of Northumberland is sufficient testimony to the difficulties faced by those who attempted to impose norms of behaviour considered alien by the majority of the working classes.

Finally, however much the social elites may have wished to eradicate sports deemed inappropriate for a civilised society, historians of sport now recognise more clearly than they once did that, except in isolated cases, the normal methods of policing were invariably too ineffective to remove speedily and completely those elements of their traditional sporting culture which the working classes were particularly determined to retain. Significantly, the suppression of the great street football occasions at Derby and Newark-on-Trent in the later 1840s was effected not by the regular police force but by the army and a force of special constables. And although officers from the Metropolitan police force were responsible for the eradication of bullrunning at Stamford in the late 1830s and of mass football matches at Twickenham and Richmond in Surrey in 1840, neither they nor anyone else succeeded in stopping street football elsewhere in Surrey – at East Mousley and Hampton Wick, Hampton and Kingston-upon-Thames – until the late 1850s or 1860s (Reid, 1988: 229; Flett, 1989: 256).

Without the necessary range of empirical evidence to confirm it, and shorn of many of the explanatory props initially advanced in its support, more recent historians of sport are reluctant to endorse the once broadly accepted view – that levels of participation in sport declined so dramatically from the later decades of the eighteenth century that by the second quarter of the nineteenth century little was left of a formerly vibrant mass sporting culture. According to current consensus, sport was more extensively played and watched in mid-nineteenth century Britain than earlier students of popular culture have been inclined to assume. The notion of an almost total collapse of sport, it is now believed, rested on an incomplete and distorted selection of evidence and on an interpretation of the Industrial Revolution which has since been discarded in favour of one that sees the process of initial industrial take-off as evolutionary rather than revolutionary in pace and regional rather than nationwide in scale and implication.

3
The 'revolution' in sport

Whatever happened in the decades immediately preceding the Victorian era, there is no doubt that the period between the mid-nineteenth century and the outbreak of the First World War was characterised by a notable transformation in the scale and nature of Britain's sporting culture. Recently, it is true, sport historians have tended to diminish the sharpness of the contrast previously drawn between the sporting worlds of the early nineteenth and early twentieth centuries. Subsumed within the Victorian and Edwardian sporting 'revolution' were numerous elements of continuity from an earlier age; their existence goes far towards explaining why modern versions of traditional sports like folk football and prize-fighting were able to spread so rapidly (Holt, 1988: 70–2; 1989: 57–73; Shipley, 1989: 90; Sandiford, 1994: 19).

Playing and watching sport was common to all social classes in the eighteenth century and, as shown in chapter 1, remained so throughout the first half of the nineteenth century. The number of people involved in sport certainly increased in the course of the second half of the nineteenth and early twentieth centuries; but as late as Edwardian times sport spectating, and particularly playing, was still the minority interest it had always been. On the eve of the First World War no more than one in twenty of all males aged 15–39 actively participated in soccer. Liverpool, with a population of over half a million, had just 224 cricket clubs in 1890 and 212 soccer clubs in 1912: Birmingham, with around 400,000 inhabitants, just 214 cricket clubs in 1880 (Vamplew, 1988a: 12). At the peak of their popularity soccer clubs in the Stirling region of Victorian Scotland attracted less than 20 per cent of all males in the age groups most likely to play, and cricket clubs only 10–15 per cent. In the sports of bowling, curling, cycling, golf, lawn tennis, quoiting and rugby the figure was rarely above 5 per cent and in most cases considerably lower. While occasional sporting events like Highland Games gatherings, horserace meetings and regattas sometimes drew crowds far in excess of the populations of the local communities, even that most popular of all the major, regularly offered sports, soccer, only attracted attendances as large as 10–20 per cent of the total number of males resident in the immediate locality (Tranter, 1987b: 306–7).

In Victorian and Edwardian no less than in Georgian times, moreover, there were numerous examples of sports which decreased rather than increased in popularity; among them professional athletics, the Scottish sport of shinty, an early form of hockey similar to the Irish game of hurling, and professional rowing. It would be quite wrong to suppose that the history of sport in late nineteenth- and early twentieth-century Britain was one of general, continuous expansion. Most sports, subject to vagaries of fashion and competition from alternative recreations in what was a more restricted market for sport than we sometimes imagine, remained as prone as sport had always been to periods of at least temporary contraction (Tranter, 1989b: 195–9; 1990c: 365–78).

Nor must we exaggerate the penchant of Victorian and Edwardian sport for commercialisation, codification and institutionalisation. Sports like cricket, horseracing, pedestrianism, prize-fighting and rowing had a long history of mass spectating, profit-seeking promoters, paid performers, stake-money contests and gambling (Brailsford, 1982; 1991: 54–65; Vamplew, 1989: 215; Sandiford, 1994: 26–9). Written rules (or laws) of conduct and play first appeared in bowls in 1670, in cricket in 1727, in golf and prize-fighting in the 1740s and in curling in 1795; and in the cases of cricket, curling and golf were nationwide in scope long before the middle of the nineteenth century. Governing bodies, with the power to frame and implement rules and arrange competitions, originated in horseracing in 1751 or 1752 (the Jockey Club), in golf in 1754 (the St Andrews' Society of Golfers, subsequently the Royal and Ancient), in cricket in 1787 (the Marylebone Cricket Club) and in curling in 1838 (the Grand Caledonian Curling Club, from 1843 the Royal Caledonian). The first formally constituted golf club, the Company of Edinburgh Golfers, was founded at Leith in 1744. By the mid-1850s there were eighteen golf clubs in Scotland. A curling club is known to have existed in the Perthshire parish of Muthill from at least as early as 1739. The first cricket club, at Hambledon, was formed in 1767 and by the 1830s, despite its less favourable climate, even Scotland had as many as a dozen active cricket clubs. In the course of the 1830s the largely working-class sport of quoiting was also beginning to develop formal club and competitive structures.

The sharpness of the contrast between the sporting cultures of the late eighteenth and early twentieth centuries is further blurred by the incompleteness of the Victorian and Edwardian trend towards codification and institutionalisation. As illustrated by the experience of Northumberland mining communities, in some regions and sports the adoption of standardised, written rules, club structures and formalised league and cup competitions was long delayed and at the end of the nineteenth century still far from complete. Among the miners of east Northumberland the codification and institutionalisation of soccer dates only from 1882; and as late as 1914 half of all teams were neither affiliated to the Northumberland Football Association nor involved in leagues. Many soccer teams were established only for special occasions and many others, chiefly because of financial problems, lacked the organisational stability to survive for more than brief periods (Metcalfe, 1982: 1988, 270-1, 275). A similar pattern of institutional fragility has been documented for the Stirling region of Scotland. There, in sports like angling, bowling, curling, cycling and golf, where middle-class participants were predominant and financial provision accordingly relatively regular and generous, institutional structures were comparatively durable. By contrast, in the sports of boatracing, cricket, harrying, Highland Games, quoiting and soccer, where there was greater reliance on working-class support and the necessary finance was more difficult to provide, they were more often short-lived (Tranter, 1990b: 199–201; 1990c: 379–84).

Important though it undoubtedly is to acknowledge the existence of continuities, the fact remains, however, that the fundamental characteristics of late Victorian and Edwardian sport were very different from those of the early Victorian period. In less than fifty years the number of sports and the numbers playing and watching sport increased dramatically, the social composition of participants and the spatial parameters of the sports they practised substantially widened, codification, institutionalisation, commercialism and professionalism became widespread for the first time, and the timing of sporting activity radically altered. While none of these developments was entirely novel to the Victorian and Edwardian periods, the pace at which they occurred was wholly unprecedented. In demonstrating the similarities with earlier sporting cultures, we must not lose sight of the fact that, in essence, the sporting culture of late nineteenth- and early twentieth-century Britain was quite unlike anything that preceded it (Lowerson, 1993: 3). Sport, in its modern, organised, commercialised and extensive form, was truly an 'invention' of the Victorian and Edwardian age.

One of the clearest signs of this 'revolution' in sporting practice was the dramatic increase in the range of sports available and in the numbers of people who played and watched them. In the 1860s and 1870s the separate sports of rugby and soccer emerged from folk football. In the 1880s and 1890s prize-fighting was displaced by amateur and professional boxing under Marquis of Queensberry rules. New sports like badminton, croquet, cycling, field hockey, lawn tennis, mountaineering, table tennis and yachting were introduced. Older sports like bowls, curling and golf, previously barely noticeable, were transformed into large-scale activities. The sports of angling, cricket, foxhunting and horseracing, which had been more widely practised, soared in popularity. In Scotland the number of deer forests rose from 28 in 1839 to 183 in 1912, covering over a third of the total land area in the five west Highland counties where the sport of deerstalking was concentrated. Between 1870 and 1914 the number of game shooting licences increased by almost a fifth from 45,914 to 54,701. The number of foxhunting packs rose from 28 in 1837 to 178 in 1911 and the number of anglers from 50,000 in 1878 to over 250,000 on the eve of the First World War.

In 1910 it has been estimated that there were between 450,000 and 650,000 soccer players in England and Scotland (Murray: 1994, 44): in 1914 the All-England Croquet Association had nearly 3,000 members and there were more than 600,000 crown green bowlers in northern England alone (Lowerson: 1988, 105;

1989b: 17; 1993: 32, 38, 103, 113). In the 1850s and 1860s 161 new horserace meetings were established. By the 1890s even minor horserace meetings regularly attracted daily attendances of 10,000–15,000. At more important meetings attendances averaged 20,000–30,000 and at major Bank Holiday events 70,000–80,000 (Huggins, 1987: 109; Vamplew, 1988a: 13).

Average daily attendances at English first-class county cricket matches rose from 2,000–3,000 in the 1840s and 4,000 in the 1860s to between 8,000 and 24,000, depending on the county and the importance of the match, in the early 1900s. By the 1890s some Lancashire League cricket clubs were regularly attracting crowds of 6,000 and even small village teams often drew up to 1,000 spectators (Sandiford: 1994, 112, 115, 119–20). In Scotland attendances at Highland Games gatherings ranged from 2,000-3,000 at the more modest to 20,000–30,000 at the most prestigious and at challenge matches between the country's leading quoiters from 200-300 to 2,000 or more. In Northern Union rugby crowds at league fixtures occasionally reached 10,000 and at cup finals varied between 8,000 and 32,000 (Vamplew, 1988b: 66). But it was in soccer that the growth of spectating was most spectacular. In the 1860s, when it first emerged as a separate sport, players probably outnumbered spectators. Beginning in the 1880s there was an extraordinary transformation. Between 1875–84 and 1905–14 average attendances at FA cup finals rose from 4,900 to 79,300 in England and from 8,550 to 51,000 in Scotland. Between 1889–90 and 1913–14 attendances at First Division English Football League matches rose from an average of 4,600 to 23,100. By 1909 in England alone around one million people watched soccer on Saturday afternoons (Vamplew, 1988b: 4, 63, 323–4; Murray, 1994: 26, 28).

With the dramatic increase in the numbers who played and watched came an equally dramatic widening in the geographic and social range of sport. In the course of the Victorian and Edwardian eras most of the major sports were transformed from purely local to national and in some cases even international activities. National championships were first held in amateur athletics in 1865, in amateur boxing in 1880 (England) and 1910–11 (Scotland and Wales), in professional boxing in 1909 and at some weights even earlier, in bowling in 1894 (Scotland) and 1905

(England) and in angling and archery in 1906. Open championships were instituted for golf in 1860 and lawn tennis in 1877. In horseracing the transition from local to national sport began in the late 1830s and was virtually complete by the late 1860s. In cricket it began in the 1840s with the formation of peripatetic clubs like I Zingari and professional touring teams such as William Clarke's All-England XI; it was consolidated in the second half of the century by the emergence of a first-class county championship. In curling it dates back to the inaugural national bonspiel of 1846–7.

Cricket sent its first professional teams to North America in 1859, Australia in 1861, South Africa in 1888 and the Caribbean in 1894. An Australian aboriginal cricket team toured England in 1868. Ten years later the first fully representative Australian side arrived, followed in the 1880s by teams representing India and in 1900 by the West Indies. In 1898 an Imperial Bowling Association was established to promote links between bowlers in Britain, Australia and Canada. In 1901 London hosted the first official international bowling match, between England and Australia, and in 1903 a home international bowling championship was instituted. Lawn tennis began its Davis Cup in 1900; the first official rugby international, England versus Scotland, was played in 1871; the first official soccer international, England versus Scotland, in 1872; and the first amateur soccer international, England versus Ireland, in 1906. Amateur soccer teams began to play in Europe in 1890 and professional soccer teams in 1900, though it was not until 1908 that the English FA agreed to send out a fully representative national eleven. A Canadian soccer team toured Britain in 1888, a German team came to play an English amateur eleven in 1901 and in 1910 a British professional soccer team toured South Africa for the first time.

In the case of rowing, where hostility to professionalism led to a decline in the number of active working-class participants, the widening geography of competition was accompanied by a narrowing in the social composition of participation (Wigglesworth, 1986). But this was not typical. In most sports there was at least a modest trend towards socially more diverse patterns of involvement. Foxhunting and game shooting spread from the landowning elites to the urban upper middle class, cycling from the professional upper middle class to humble white-collar and skilled workers, and institutionalised forms of angling and golf from the middle classes to working-class artisans (Lowerson, 1989b: 19; 1993, 32–4, 38, 117, 142–4). In horseracing the ownership of stud farms, once the prerogative of wealthy landowners, was increasingly taken over by the *nouveaux riches* from commerce and industry (Huggins, 1987: 104). Amateur boxing, initially a wholly middle-class recreation, was transformed in the 1890s into a popular working-class sport (Shipley, 1989: 91). From the early 1870s the hitherto essentially middle-class pastime of rugby attracted increasing numbers of working-class participants and by 1900, particularly in the manufacturing and mining areas of south Wales and the English Midlands and north, was a well-established working-class game (Dunning and Sheard, 1979: 142–4; Lowerson, 1993: 83).

In cricket, too, the extent of working-class involvement grew rapidly from the 1870s and 1880s, so much so that by the end of the century organised, competitive forms of cricket were an important ingredient in the culture of working-class males (Tranter, 1987b: 309–10). It was in soccer, however, that the greatest change in the social composition of participation occurred. Down to the early 1870s an active involvement in the new game of soccer was restricted solely to middle-class men and students at the elite public schools and universities. By the close of the decade it already had a substantial following among skilled workers and by 1914 was an overwhelmingly working-class sport (Mason, 1980: 22–3, 31–2, 152–3; Tranter, 1987b: 310; Murray, 1994: 31, 33).

Perhaps the most novel feature of the Victorian and Edwardian sporting 'revolution' was the reduction and concentration in the periods of time during which organised forms of sport were watched and played. To accommodate the new chronology of leisure time imposed on players and spectators by the requirements of a modern, capitalist economy for regular hours of work and an increasingly common Monday to Friday working week, the majority of sports were forced to restrict their availability to Saturday afternoons. Horseracing and first-class county cricket, both of which continued to rely heavily on the financial support of a landed elite whose patterns of work and leisure differed little from those of an earlier age, were among the very few major sports able to resist the trend and persist with the prolonged and irregular time-schedules which had been typical of sport in pre-industrial times (Brailsford, 1991: 66–122).

Within its more constricted time-span sport became noticeably more commercial and professional than before. Grounds were enclosed, stadia were constructed, spectators were charged for admission, the numbers of professional sportsmen and other paid employees greatly increased and, to meet the costs of all this, more and more sporting organisations found it necessary to adopt limited liability company status. Nowhere were these developments better illustrated than in horseracing. Before the mid-1870s spectators at horserace meetings were rarely charged for watching, stud fees never exceeded fifty guineas and, with only occasional exceptions like Nat Flatman, jockeys were little more than paid servants. By 1914 the sport had been transformed. Stud fees for the best stallions could reach as high as 600 guineas. There were some 400 full-time professional jockeys and apprentice jockeys. All the major venues were enclosed courses which charged spectators for admission. All were limited liability companies with initial issues of share capital ranging from £26,000, in the case of Sandown Park (1885), to £34,000 for Haydock Park (1898) and £80,000 for Newbury (1906). And all had spent lavishly on employing staff, increasing prize money and improving facilities. At Stockton, for example, considerable sums were spent on improvements to the grandstands and parade ring, seventy horse boxes and a stable yard with dormitories for the stable lads were constructed, and between 1860 and 1893 total prize money was raised from £1,100 to £6,250. The amount of prize money available in horseracing increased from £413,066 in 1882 to £511,734 in 1910 (Vamplew, 1976: 38–48, 191–2; 1988b, 56–7, 103; 1989, 216; Huggins, 1987: 107–9).

To varying degrees, what happened in horseracing was replicated in many other sports. Gate-money cricket, which began in the eighteenth century, expanded dramatically from the 1840s. In 1885 the Surrey County Cricket Club had just 230 members and a total income of less than £500. By 1899 its membership had risen to 4,000 and its receipts from cricket alone to £13,593. In 1910 there were over 200 first-class cricket professionals and several hundred others employed on county groundstaffs, with league clubs or as coaches in public schools (Mandle, 1973: 3; Vamplew, 1980: 5; 1988b, 54; Sandiford: 1994, 69). The number of professional soccer players in Scotland rose from 560 in 1893–4 to 1,754 in 1913–14 and in England from 1,092 in 1889 to around 7,000 in 1914, of whom about 2,500 were full time. By 1913–14 the annual income of eight English first division clubs averaged £19,269, sufficient to permit massive expenditures on ground improvements. In 1909 Manchester United spent almost £36,000 on new stands while expenditure on improvements to Goodison Park (Everton), between 1906 and 1909, and Ewood Park (Blackburn Rovers), in the decade after 1905, totalled £41,000 and £33,000 respectively. Even in the less well-supported sport of rugby league a club like Oldham had spent £8,000 on its ground by 1906 and the Bradford club had facilities valued at £25,000 (Vamplew, 1988b: 63–5, 210). Similar outlays were common in the sport of golf. In the 1890s the Royal Liverpool Club invested £8,000 in a new clubhouse; in 1914 the Royal Automobile Club a massive £75,000 on a golf course at Epsom. On the eve of World War I there were around a thousand golf professionals and annual expenditures on golf were estimated at about £700,0000, of which £600,000 was spent on golf balls alone.

Because of the imprecise and fragmentary nature of the surviving quantitative data, it is impossible to determine exactly the overall amount of capital invested in sport and the number of people it employed. One contemporary suggested that in 1895 expenditures on sport were already the equivalent of 3 per cent of total gross national product, though this should be regarded as little more than a crude estimate. The number of men paid to play or coach sport was certainly small. But the number employed to service the sport industry – as boatmen and yachting hands, caddies and greenkeepers, groundsmen and turnstile attendants, golf course architects, gamekeepers, hunt servants and the like, and indirectly as employees of the industries and trades which supplied sport with its stadia, playing equipment and clothing – was very much larger. By the early 1890s as many as 10,000 people depended on horseracing for a living. Between 1851 and 1911 the number of gamekeepers rose from 9,000 to 23,000. By 1912 there were over 800 hunt servants and, in England and Wales alone, at least 10,000 golf caddies (Vamplew, 1988b: 54, 322; Lowerson, 1993: 191–2, 198, 225).

Typical of the many firms which emerged to satisfy the burgeoning demand for sports equipment was that of William

Shillcock which, at its peak, was selling between 40,000 and 50,000 footballs a year. In Glasgow the number of football outfitters rose from eight in 1885 to twenty in 1900: in the town of Alnwick the output of flyfishing rods from 800 a year in the mid-1880s to 3,500 a year a decade later. By 1914 160 firms were manufacturing golf clubs and 74 manufacturing golf balls. Most were small concerns. But a few like the Rubastic Company, which employed 5,000 workers to make seamless golf balls in a new £650,000 factory at Southall, and the All British Boot Works at Northampton, which produced 250,000 golf shoes and brogues a year, were substantial in scale. Between 1870 and 1914, 260 books on golf and 237 books on guns and shooting were published; 30 volumes of the Badminton series of books on sport appeared between 1885 and 1914 and 35 editions of Walton's *Compleat Angler* between 1870 and 1902 (Vamplew, 1988b: 55; Lowerson, 1993: 229, 238–9, 254–5). Sport obviously became a major industry during the Victorian and Edwardian periods.

To cope with its new scale and sophistication, significant alterations were required to the regulatory and organisational structures of sport. Standardised, written rules of play rapidly became the norm rather than the exception. New laws of bowling were compiled by W. W. Mitchell in 1849. The Jockey Club's *Rules of Racing*, already voluntarily accepted by racecourse committees by the 1850s, were made compulsory in 1870. The Marquess of Queensberry rules of boxing were drawn up in 1867. Wingfield's rules of lawn tennis were adopted and disseminated by the MCC and the All England Croquet Club between 1875 and 1882. Common codes of rules were first published for field hockey in 1883, for badminton in 1887 and for shinty in 1893.

At the micro level the 'revolution' in organisational structures involved the formation of clubs on a scale never before experienced. Between 1838 and 1900 the number of clubs affiliated to the Royal Caledonian Curling Club rose from 36 to 655, incorporating some 20,000 curlers. Mid-nineteenth-century England had just one golf club, at Blackheath, and as late as 1879 there were still only seventy-two golf clubs in the whole of Britain, of which all but twenty were in Scotland. During the boom years of the 1890s and early 1900s 704 new clubs were established, almost three-quarters of them in England. By 1912 the total number of golf clubs in England had risen to 1,200 (Lowerson, 1989a: 125, 188).

Club-based angling began in Sheffield in the 1860s. At its formation in 1869 the Sheffield Anglers' Association already boasted 180 affiliated clubs and 8,000 members. By 1914 the number of affiliated clubs had increased to 500 and the number of members to 21,291. Similar developments occurred in other cities – in the case of London, where the Federation of Angling Associations represented 620 individual clubs by 1900, on an even larger scale (Lowerson, 1988: 113–15; 1989b, 19).

In soccer the process of club formation began in England in 1857 (the Sheffield Football Club) and in Scotland in 1867 (the Queens Park Football Club). By 1906 116 clubs were affiliated to the Scottish Football Association and by 1914 the number of professional soccer clubs in England had risen to 158 and the number of junior clubs to over 12,000 (Vamplew, 1988b: 128; Fishwick, 1989: 1, 26). The first rugby club was established at Blackheath in 1863. Between 1871 and 1893 the number of clubs affiliated to the English Rugby Football Union increased from 32 to 481 before falling to 244 in 1903 as a result of competition from soccer and the formation of the Northern Rugby Football Union in 1895. In croquet the first formally constituted clubs date back to the 1850s, in shinty to the 1870s and in amateur boxing to the 1880s. The first lawn tennis club was set up at Leamington Spa in 1872. By 1900 three hundred clubs were affiliated to the Lawn Tennis Association: by 1914 there were around a thousand (Holt, 1989: 126). The number of clubs represented by the Amateur Athletics Association rose from 45 in 1880 to 502 in 1914, the English Hockey Association from 200 in 1900 to 518 in 1914, the English Bowling Association from 95 in 1907 to 237 in 1914 and the Badminton Association from 20 in 1898 to 263 in 1912 (Crump, 1989: 44–5; Lowerson, 1993: 85, 102, 109, 114).

John Lowerson has suggested that the process of club formation in sport was primarily a feature of the last quarter of the nineteenth century (Lowerson, 1993: 96). Others believe that it was already well under way by the third quarter of the century (Bailey, 1978: 61). At the local level in particular a good deal more research is needed before the validity of these competing claims can be properly assessed. Such limited evidence as is currently available, however, indicates that the timing of club formation varied considerably from sport to sport and that generalisation is unwise. In the Stirling region of Scotland, for example, institutional structures were already widespread in the sports of curling and quoiting by the end of the second quarter of the nineteenth century. In other sports – angling, boatracing, bowls, competitive pedestrianism, cricket, Highland Games and live pigeon shooting – they became common only in the third quarter of the century, and in the sports of amateur athletics, clay pigeon and glass ball shooting, cycling, golf, harrying, lawn tennis, rugby and soccer not until the final quarter of the century. On the other hand, in all sports, once begun, the pace of the trend towards institutionalisation was rapid. In Stirling and its immediate environs the number of curling clubs rose from 25 in the 1830s and 51 in the 1840s to roughly 100 in the 1870s, angling clubs from 1 in the 1840s to 28 in the 1880s, bowling clubs from 5 in the 1840s to 43 in the 1890s, cricket clubs from 5 in the 1840s to 173 in the 1870s, quoiting clubs from 21 in the 1830s and 13 in the 1840s to 45 in the 1890s and golf clubs from 1 in the 1850s to 31 in the 1890s. In the 1840s the region hosted just 2 Highland Games gatherings; by the 1870s 30. Between the 1870s and the 1890s the number of cycling clubs rose from 4 to 30, lawn tennis clubs from 3 to 13, amateur athletics meetings from 6 to 33 and soccer clubs from 66 to a staggering 566 (Tranter, 1990b: 189-90, 192).

At the macro level the organisational 'revolution' in sport was reflected in the widespread establishment of governing bodies to oversee the rules and organise and run competitions. In England national associations were formed for rugby union in 1871, amateur athletics in 1879, amateur boxing in 1880, amateur rowing in 1882, cycling in 1885, lawn tennis in 1888, badminton in 1893, croquet and field hockey in 1896, table tennis in 1901, angling and bowling in 1903 and amateur crown green bowling in 1907. MCC control over first-class cricket grew to such an extent that by the Edwardian era it was responsible for the English county championship, England's official overseas tours and domestic Test matches. The establishment of the English Football Association in 1863 was followed by the formation of regional associations for Sheffield (1867), Birmingham (1875), Staffordshire and Surrey (1877), Berkshire, Buckinghamshire, Cheshire and Lancashire

(1878), Durham and Northumberland (1879), Cleveland, Lincolnshire and Norfolk (1881), London, Liverpool, Shropshire, Northamptonshire, Nottinghamshire, Sussex, Walsall and Scarborough and the East Riding (1882), Derbyshire, Essex, Kent and Middlesex (1883), Cambridgeshire, South Hampshire and Dorset (1884) and Somerset and Suffolk (1885). An International Football Association Board, with two representatives from each of the home countries, was set up in 1886 and in 1906, two years after its foundation, England joined FIFA. In 1907, as a belated response to the legalisation of professionalism, an English Amateur Football Association, which remained independent of the English FA until 1914, was instituted. Similar developments occurred in Scotland and Wales where, among others, national associations were established in the case of the former for rugby and soccer (1873), shinty (1893), bowls and cricket (1902) and amateur soccer (1909), and in the case of the latter for soccer (1876), rugby (1881) and bowls (1904).

With the creation of governing bodies came a proliferation of regional and national league and cup competitions. In 1895, for instance, shinty set up its first national inter-club tournament, the Camanachd Cup, and English cricket its Minor Counties Championship. In northern and Midland regions of England, especially, the closing years of the nineteenth century were marked by a veritable explosion of league and cup competitions for cricket clubs: a Heavy Woollen District Cup at Batley in Yorkshire (1883), a Birmingham and District League (1888), a North Staffordshire and District League (1889), a Lancashire League (1890), a Huddersfield League (1892), the Central Lancashire, Ribblesdale and North Yorkshire and South Durham leagues (1893) and a Saddlesworth and District League (1898) (Sandiford, 1994: 55–6). In Scotland the Western Union and North of Scotland cricket leagues were begun in 1893, a Border League in 1895 and the Scottish County Championship in 1902. Challenge cups for rugby union clubs were introduced in Yorkshire in 1877, Durham and Northumberland in 1880 and Cumberland in 1882 and an inter-county championship in 1888–9.

But it was in soccer that the development of competitive structures began earliest and proceeded furthest. A Scottish FA Cup was started in 1873, a Welsh FA Cup in 1877 and a Scottish

League in 1890; an English FA Cup in 1871, an English FA Amateur Cup in 1893 and the (English) Football League in 1888. Among the myriad more important local leagues that had emerged in England by 1914 were the Northern League (1889–90), the Southern League (1894), the London and I Zingari leagues (1895), the Isthmian League (1905), the Amateur Football Alliance (1906) and the Athenian League (1912). Even in the mining districts of east Northumberland, where organised, codified forms of soccer did not appear until the 1880s, once begun the spread of league and cup competitions was rapid (Metcalfe, 1988: 269, 271, 273). On the eve of World War I the range and depth of league and cup structures in soccer was unparalleled in any other sport (Murray, 1994: 49).

In recent years there has been considerable debate over the way in which this new culture of codified, institutionalised sport was spread. Some scholars have favoured a simple downwards social diffusionist model. According to this model, organised forms of sport originated in the most prestigious of the elite public schools. From these schools they passed first to public schools of more modest status and, except during the 1860s and 1870s when the predominant flow was sometimes from the universities to the schools (Chandler, 1988a: 20–1; 1991, 173–4), to the ancient universities and then to the new civic universities, the more ambitious grammar schools and outwards into adult upper and middle-class society. From middle-class society, either through the influence of emulation or the proselytising endeavours of former public schoolboys and university alumni, they eventually spread to the working classes (Mandle: 1973, 512–14; Walvin, 1978: 81–96; Dunning and Sheard, 1979: 65–144; Allison, 1980, 10; Mangan, 1983: 313, 320).

There is enough evidence to suggest that the downwards diffusionist model is not entirely without foundation. It was, after all, ex-public schoolboys and university men who instigated the formation of the English Football Association, devised the first common set of rules for sports like rugby and soccer, set up the first athletics clubs and the Amateur Athletics Association and dominated Scottish rugby union (Crump, 1989: 44, 48; Holt, 1989: 83, 85; Mason, 1989b, 146). In the spread of organised forms of amateur rowing from the public schools to the universities of Oxford and Cambridge and of cycling from the aristocracy and upper middle class to white-collar workers and artisans there are obvious indications that in some sports at least elements of a social diffusionist process were at work. The transition of amateur boxing from a middle-class to a working-class sport owed at least something to clubs established by the churches and university settlements (Shipley, 1989: 83). As Gareth Williams notes, implausible though it is to claim that *all* sports clubs were created by the sons of local squires or factory owners returning home from school or university, there are numerous instances where this did happen. Former pupils of schools like Galashiels Academy and Kelso High played a significant part in the diffusion of rugby in the Scottish borders. The Edinburgh Academicals club was founded by former pupils of the Edinburgh Academy, the Sheffield FC by old boys of the Sheffield Collegiate school, York FC by former pupils of the city's St Peter's school and Manchester FC by men who had attended the universities of Oxford or Cambridge and schools such as Cheltenham, Edinburgh Academy, Fettes, Manchester Grammar, Rugby and Uppingham. The Aston Villa, Bolton, Burnley and Everton soccer clubs, the Bramley and Wakefield Trinity rugby league clubs, the Northampton rugby union clubs and rugby union clubs like Penydarren Church Juniors and Dowlais St Illtyd's in Merthyr and St Peter's Stars and St Paul's United in Llanelli were among many whose origins lay in church or other religious organisations. The popularity of rugby among the working classes of south Wales likewise owed much to the promotional efforts of newly formed colleges and revived grammar schools such as Lampeter, Llandovery, Cowbridge, Brecon and Monmouth and the pioneering dynamism and administrative skills of the solicitors, surveyors, businessmen and other professional men who retained control of Welsh rugby long after its players and spectators had become predominantly working class (Holt, 1989: 84; Williams, 1989: 309–11, 314, 319–20). That former public school and university men made some contribution to the spread of sport among the working classes is further confirmed by evidence for Lancashire and Yorkshire in the late 1870s, where spatial variations in the preference for rugby or soccer depended at least in part on whether the local elite attended a rugby-playing or soccer-playing institution (Russell, 1988: 193–4).

To other historians, however, such examples of the social diffusionist process at work are less impressive than the model's obvious
limitations. One problem is that many of the sports which became
popular with adult middle-class males – badminton, bowls, croquet, golf and lawn tennis – were little practised at school or university (Lowerson, 1993: 100). Another is that many of the sports
popular with the upper and middle classes – badminton, croquet,
cycling, golf, lawn tennis, mountaineering and yachting, for
example – were never extensively taken up by the working classes.
In part, of course, this was merely a consequence of constraints of
space, the high cost of providing the required facilities or the
inability of many potential working-class consumers to find the
necessary time and money. But, for reasons discussed below, it also
reflected a reluctance or outright hostility on the part of at least
some members of the public school and university-educated elite
to the spread of the new sports among the lower orders. The opposition of many Anglican churchmen to Welsh rugby and the unwill-
ingness of local authorities, land and colliery owners, church,
school and university organisations to assist miners' sport in south
Northumberland are clear indications that an elite education did
not always foster attitudes sympathetic to the diffusion of sport
down the social hierarchy (Metcalfe, 1982: 480, 482, 488–91;
Williams, 1988: 133).

A third problem with the downwards social diffusionist model
is the assumption that working-class sport was always an exact
copy of elite initiatives and had no independent life of its own.
The reality was very different. As the case of the Northumberland
miners illustrates, working-class sports were often self-initiated
and owed little to elite example or imposition (Metcalfe, 1982;
1990: 356, 361). The adoption of written rules of play and institutional structures in the sport of quoiting was due entirely to the
efforts of its own predominantly working-class participants (Tranter, 1990a: 60). Some sports, like cricket, already had a substantial working-class following long before the emergence of the
public school games cult and therefore cannot easily be fitted into
a social diffusionist model (Lowerson, 1993: 82). Rugby may have
been the variant of folk football most favoured in the elite schools
and universities of Scotland but, outside the Border counties, it
was soccer that was preferred by the nation's working classes.

Religious organisations may have been the locus around which many working-class cricket and soccer teams were based but most of the initiative for their formation came not from those who instituted and managed such organisations but from the membership itself. As the profusion of neighbourhood and work-based clubs and teams confirms, the impetus for the spread of organised sport to working-class men came as much from below as from above and was by no means simply an inevitable, later consequence of middle-class initiative and example (Bailey, 1978: 138–9, 146; Holt, 1989: 138–40, 150, 153).

Perhaps the main weakness in the social diffusionist model, however, is its failure to give sufficient weight to the many other factors which helped determine the way in which organised sport was dispersed: the contribution of 'exiled' Scottish businessmen and returning holidaymakers to the spread of golf from Scotland to England and from coastal to inland locations; the part played by immigrants of *all* social classes to the growth of sport in south Wales; the influence of climate on the failure of curling to develop more extensively in England and of cricket to develop more extensively in Scotland; and the role of interest-generating league and cup competitions in accounting for working-class preferences for soccer over rugby and rugby league over rugby union (Bale, 1982: 156; Russell, 1988: 194–5; Lowerson 1989a: 188, 191; Mason, 1989b: 146; Williams, 1989: 314). More significantly still, it distracts attention from the effect of variations in economic structure on the type of sport most favoured. As a general rule, the more industrial and commercial the economy the greater the extent of organised sport and the earlier its inception. It was no accident that Britain, the first country to industrialise, was also the first country to introduce a codified, institutionalised and highly commercialised sporting culture. Differences in economic structure also had a marked influence on the popularity of individual sports. Sports like lawn tennis and amateur soccer were strongest in the more commercial and rural areas of southern and suburban Britain. Sports like professional boxing and professional soccer, on the other hand, were chiefly associated with the more heavily populated urban industrial areas of the north and midlands and their success or failure integrally dependent on the prosperity of the economies they inhabited (Bale, 1982: 23–5, 29, 48, 63, 95, 150; 1989: 53–7).

Above all, undue emphasis on the social diffusionist interpretation of sport's dispersal obscures the influence exerted by distance, community size and, particularly, cultural boundaries. As John Bale has demonstrated, in part the spatial dispersal of professional soccer was determined simply by distance from the place in which it first originated: the greater the distance from its 'culture hearth' the later its adoption. Thus, professional soccer began at Darwen in Lancashire in the late 1870s, spread first to the neighbouring towns of Blackburn and Bolton in 1880 and Preston in 1882 and thereafter to an ever-widening area beyond Lancashire to the south-east and north-east. In south-west England and south Wales, where larger communities adopted it earlier than smaller, there is also evidence of a positive correlation between the spread of professional soccer and community size. Even so, the influence of community size and proximity to the original 'culture hearth' on the geographic diffusion of professional soccer should not be exaggerated. Outside south-west England and south Wales there is nothing to suggest that the sport gradually percolated down the hierarchy of community size. Before the mid-1880s smaller urban communities often adopted professional soccer earlier than larger ones and, on balance, the direction of dispersal was up rather than down the urban hierarchy. After the mid-1880s, except in the sense that a minimum population size was necessary to sustain it, in most regions the spread of professionalism in soccer bore no obvious relationship to the size of communities, smaller towns frequently adopting it at the same time as larger. Just as in south Wales, where proximity to the rugby-playing counties of Hereford, Gloucester, Somerset and Devon helps to account for the preference for rugby over soccer, so proximity to the 'culture hearth' had a significant influence on the spread of professional soccer in the counties of Durham and Northumberland and, at least initially, was probably the dominant impulse on its diffusion in most regions of the country.

But at a wider, national level its influence is harder to detect. At a time when an awareness of new sports and new forms of sport must have been more or less instantaneously available to all parts of the country, it is unlikely that distance from its 'culture hearth' alone can explain why the spread of professional soccer to southern England was so long delayed and why, despite its proximity to the initial loci of professional soccer in Lancashire and Sheffield, the West Riding textile district of Yorkshire was the last major industrial area to take up the game. The process of diffusion in sports like soccer was perhaps influenced more by variations in cultural structures and values and the variety of demographic, economic, ethnic, political and religious forces which contributed to their persistence. In the preference of southern England for amateurism over professionalism, for rugby union over professional soccer and rugby league and for playing the game rather than winning, the power of the public school and university variant of the games cult no doubt played a part. Yet, as the diversity of local preferences for soccer or rugby in Lancashire and Yorkshire reveals, cultural divergences between regions like the West Riding textile and south Yorkshire coal and steel belts require a more complex explanation. In the failure of soccer to spread from Lancashire to the West Riding of Yorkshire in the 1880s lay a cultural dichotomy which owed as much to the physical barrier imposed by the Pennines and other long-standing economic, political and social determinants of regional divergence as it did to variations in the spatial distribution of individuals and institutions whose attitudes to sport had been moulded by exposure to the public school games ethic (Bale, 1978: 191–2, 194–6; 1982: 25, 63; 1989, 57–67; Russell, 1988: 195–6; Arnold, 1989: 319; Huggins, 1989: 302). The impact of cultural factors was itself sometimes overriden by other forces. In the West Riding textile district, for example, while alterations to the cultural environment brought about by 'nationalising' agencies like education and the press clearly played their part, the eventual displacement of rugby by soccer may have owed most to the latter's greater potential for generating revenue (Arnold, 1989: 320, 322–8, 330).

The debate over the influences most responsible for the way the new forms of sport were dispersed remains far from resolved. More research is urgently required to assess more precisely the relative significance of each of the numerous factors involved. But it is already evident that an explanation which relies too heavily on a downwards social diffusionist model is too restricted to be acceptable as an adequate description and interpretation of the spread of organised sport in Victorian and Edwardian Britain.

4

A conspiracy of the elites?

Underlying the 'revolution' which occurred in the extent and character of sporting activity during the Victorian and Edwardian eras was a complex mix of forces which made it possible for a new sporting culture to emerge. One of these was rising standards of nutrition which supplied the energy needed for more regular participation in physical recreation (Vamplew, 1988a, 11). A second was the growing availability of land on which to play, itself a combined result of the spaciousness of the new suburbs, the greater provision of public parks and playing fields by local authorities and private philanthropists and, particularly in the case of golf, the falling cost of marginal agricultural land caused by the late nineteenth-century decline in food prices (Allison, 1980: 12; Lowerson, 1989a: 191–2; 1993: 16; Sandiford, 1994: 54). A third was the continued growth of population and urbanisation which further expanded the opportunities for sport entrepreneurship and facilitated the rise of mass spectator sports like boxing, horseracing, pedestrianism and soccer (Cunningham, 1980: 36; Vamplew, 1988a: 13).

Another was the increasing size of the middle-class population – from the elites of business and the professions to the tradesmen and lower-status occupations of clerks and teachers – whose income levels and working experiences were especially conducive to participation in leisure activities (Lowerson, 1993: 5–12). Yet another was the growing ease of communication made possible by rising rates of literacy, the invention of the telegraph and the advent of cheap, mass-circulation newspapers and specialist sports publications. Together with portraits on cigarette cards and postcards, these raised the profiles and allure of sporting heroes, increased the opportunities for gambling on sporting contests, speeded the adoption of the standardised rules and practices that were so vital to the initiation of inter-regional and international sporting competitions and provided the information on venues, timing and results that was so vital to the ability of sport to attract spectators (Allison, 1980: 12; Brailsford, 1991: 88; Sandiford, 1994: 54, 136). But of all the forces which go towards explaining why the emergence of an extensive, modern sporting culture was delayed until the second half of the nineteenth century and why it appeared first in Britain the most important were the changes that occurred in industrial technology, methods of transport, hours of work and levels of real wages.

Advances in industrial technology were a critical, if often over-looked, contributor to the sporting 'revolution'. The various shooting sports could not have flourished without the availability of more efficient guns made possible by the invention of detonating chemicals, copper percussion caps, breech-loading shotguns and self-contained, central-fire cartridges. Golf owed much of its popularity to the replacement of feather-packed balls first by gutta-percha balls and later by machine-made, rubber-strip balls which extended driving distances and thus made the game more pleasurable. Lawn mowers and rollers produced the smooth playing surfaces essential for the growth of sports like bowls, cricket, golf, hockey and lawn tennis: vulcanised rubber was used to provide satisfactory tennis balls and the inner tubes for better rugby and soccer balls; innovations in methods of refining and working iron and steel produced the iron-headed clubs needed for golf, the frames for bicycles, improved ice-skates and the pavilions, grandstands and enclosed stadia required by mass spectator sports like cricket, soccer and horseracing (Allison, 1980: 11; Lowerson, 1989a: 194; Sandiford, 1994: 132, 134–6).

No less vital were the advances made in methods of transport. As the example of the mining communities of south Northumberland reminds us, transport improvements were not always immediately followed by radical changes in the way sport was practised (Metcalfe, 1982: 476). But even in south Northumberland the ultimate impact of railways, steamships and improved methods of road transport was unmistakable (Walvin, 1978: 18–30). The survival of prize-fighting into the second half of the nineteenth century owed a good deal to the ability of its supporters to evade the forces of law and order by utilising the new stagecoaches, railways and river steamers to pursue their sport in remoter locations. By the same token, the passing of the Regulation of Railways Act in 1868, which ended the provision of special trains for its spectators, contributed something to the sport's eventual decline (Vamplew, 1988b: 47; Brailsford, 1991: 88, 92). The success of the shooting and fishing sports of the Scottish Highlands was heavily dependent on the easier access provided by a combination of better roads, the introduction of sea-going paddle steamers and the extension of the railway network.

Railways facilitated the emergence of the first professional touring teams in cricket, increased the number of waterways readily accessible to anglers, stimulated the construction of golf courses by contributing to the spread of the middle-class commuter belt and helped broaden the social composition of the devotees of field sports like foxhunting by making it easier for the elite urban professional and business classes to participate. Sports as diverse as cricket, horseracing, pedestrianism and soccer were transformed from local into regional and, in some cases, national events by the effect of improved transport systems on the mobility of participants and spectators. With the coming of the transoceanic steamship and the opening of the Suez canal, a few, like cricket, even became intercontinental in their scope.

The impact of transport improvements was particularly marked in the sport of horseracing, where proximity to a railway soon became crucial to the success of a course and where, in the brief period encompassing the third quarter of the nineteenth century, the sport was transformed by the effect of rail travel on the mobility of horses, jockeys, officials and spectators from a localised activity of mediocre standard to a thoroughly commercial and professional recreation based around a calendar of major meetings drawing their participants from all parts of the country. But few sports entirely escaped the influence of transport improvements. In most cases, the geographic and social range of participation was extended. The proliferation of codified and institutionalised forms of play was encouraged. The duration of sporting contests was shortened and their timing increasingly restricted to Saturday afternoons (Allison, 1980: 11–12; Vamplew,

1988a: 11; 1988b: 47; Huggins, 1989: 313; Brailsford, 1991: 86, 93–6, 98).

To the contributions made by advances in industrial technology and transport must be added those made by the decline in the length of the average working week, and the introduction of the Saturday (or, in some service occupations, the mid-week) half-day. The former increased the amount of time (and energy) available for sport. The latter separated working hours from leisure hours more sharply than ever before and created that commonly shared period of leisure-time so essential to the development of suitably abbreviated mass participant and spectator sports. Given the independent influence exerted by occupational variations and the numerous other influences which together determine how leisure-time is used, we must not expect too close a link between the rise of organised sport and improvements in the leisure:work ratio. None the less, though more work is needed to assess its significance in detail, the existence of at least a crude correlation between socio-occupational, chronological variations in rates of participation in sport, on the one hand, and in the adoption of a shorter working week and the Saturday half-day, on the other, is indisputable. It is no coincidence that the chronology of the social diffusion of the new sporting culture – from the more prosperous middle-class groups around the mid-nineteenth century to skilled and semi-skilled manual workers and the lower middle class in the third quarter of the century and the unskilled in the late 1880s and 1890s – reflects, albeit crudely, variations in the dates at which shorter working hours and the Saturday half-day, were first achieved (Myerscough, 1974: 7; Bailey, 1978: 80–1; Walvin, 1978: 30–1, 60–8; Cunningham, 1980: 141–50; Brailsford, 1991: 100–2, 106–8). Nor is it a coincidence that it was in the country which pioneered the introduction of technologies and forms of labour organisation permissive of reductions in working hours that a modern, mass sporting culture was first established (Myerscough, 1974: 7, 9; Mason, 1980: 3).

For a sporting transformation of the kind that occurred in Victorian and Edwardian Britain to be possible one further enabling factor was required: levels of per capita real income high enough to allow large numbers of people a margin for expenditure on leisure activities. In the absence of detailed data on the spending habits of different sections of the population, and on when and how far these altered in the course of the period, the effect of real income trends on the growth of organised sport cannot be measured with any precision. But here, too, the existence of a broad correlation between levels of real income and rates of participation in sport by socio-occupational class is sufficiently well documented to confirm the significance of disposable income. Real incomes high enough to permit a substantial involvement in leisure pursuits were already available to the more prosperous sections of middle-class society by the mid-nineteenth century, hence their relatively early adoption of the new institutionalised forms of sport. Most white-collar and skilled manual workers did not enjoy such incomes until the third quarter of the century, when they too joined the sporting 'revolution': for the bulk of the semi-skilled and unskilled this did not happen until the final quarter of the century or later (Myerscough, 1974: 7; Bailey, 1978: 84; Walvin, 1978: 30–2, 60–8; Cunningham, 1980: 150–1; Vamplew, 1988b: 47–8, 50; Lowerson, 1993: 12–15). Despite winning a five-day working week as early as 1872, the coalminers of north-east England had to wait until the 1880s before their incomes were high and stable enough to enable them to embrace soccer (Huggins, 1989: 305). Boxing was just one of many sports to win an extensive working-class following only when, in the 1890s, unskilled and casual workers were able regularly to afford the sixpence or so required to watch (Shipley, 1989: 91).

However necessary they were, by themselves the various enabling forces summarised above cannot, of course, be considered a sufficient explanation for the Victorian and Edwardian 'revolution' in sport. The crucial question must be why ever-larger numbers of people chose to devote at least part of their additional income and leisure-time to sport rather than to some other form of recreation. Part of the answer may be that alternative ways of spending time and money were severely restricted by the limited range of cheap consumer goods then available and the lack of sufficiently attractive incentives to pursue other forms of cultural activity (Bailey, 1978: 84). But the principal explanation is that participation in sport was itself believed to yield a particularly valuable return. What this return was has been the subject of considerable debate.

To many historians the main reason for the growth of contemporary support for the creation of a properly codified and institutionalised sporting culture was the contribution it was thought this would make to the maintenance of social control and stability. To the extent that violent and potentially disruptive and debasing traditional working-class sports had survived the initial stage of industrial take-off the need to ensure a more ordered and temperate culture of sport among the working classes was presumably all the more urgent.

Over the years the social control explanation for the rise of organised sport has taken a number of different forms. In its earliest and crudest form of expression it argued that the new culture of sport would work to promote stability in one or other of several ways: by providing an alternative attraction to drink; by distracting men from radical politics and crime; and by encouraging a greater degree of social cohesion and understanding through the association of the different classes in shared sporting pastimes and institutions. For each of these laudable ambitions there is no difficulty in finding an abundance of supporting contemporary comment. Thus, in the words of John Burn Murdoch, patron of the Doune and Deanston Quoits Club in 1876, 'quoiting draws young men away from the dram shop'. 'Wherever cricket is widely practised, crime is very light', claimed Mr Baron Platt in an address to the grand jury at the Lancaster Assizes in 1851. 'With more curling clubs there would be fewer radical opinions and strikes among the working classes', a Mr J. T. S. Patterson of Plean insisted in 1867 (Tranter, 1989a: 240–1).

Special emphasis was given to the value of sport as a vehicle for breaking down class barriers. Following the inaugural Sheffield FA Cup Final in 1877, J. C. Shaw, the Association's president, declared his satisfaction at the fact that the Sheffield team 'was a mixed one of gentlemen of the middle classes and working men. Such meetings broke down prejudice and had a beneficial effect in cementing good feeling between all classes' (Mason, 1982: 252). 'We had some thought that the harmony and good feeling which the pleasurable excitement of bowls encourage ... would be a great means of breaking down the many partitions which divide our community with so many parties', one of the promoters of bowling in the town of Falkirk noted in 1859. Highland Games gatherings were thought to 'bring into happy alliance the rich and the poor'. Of golf it was claimed that 'no other pastime in so short a time has wielded so potent an influence on the fusion of the classes'. Cricket 'is one of the very few English sports, if not the only remaining one, in which the gentle and the simple of the land meet together for enjoyment on terms of social equality ... no game ... will endure comparison ... as a source of good feeling among men of different grades', *The Athenaeum* claimed in 1866 (Tranter, 1989a: 240–1).

From the frequency with which temperance societies, church organisations and individuals like Arnold Hills participated in the establishment of sports clubs it is clear that there were at least some contemporaries whose motives for supporting the cause of organised sport were grounded in a belief that it served to promote social stability by diverting men from drink, crime and political agitation or increasing the extent of social class intercourse. Latterly, however, even those historians who continue to explain the Victorian and Edwardian sporting 'revolution' chiefly as the result of elitist efforts to ensure social order have come to accept that the majority of sport's contemporary supporters are unlikely to have been so naive as to believe this. At a time when so much working-class sport revolved around the public house, it is difficult to believe that any but the most blinkered of contemporaries would have expected sport always to lead men away from drink and the problems associated with it (Holt, 1989: 148). In fact, many contemporary observers were convinced that sport was more likely to increase than decrease levels of drunkenness, crime and other forms of anti-social behaviour. In 1854 the Stirling Horse Races were denounced as 'an ... evil to which the violent and the vicious look forward as to a carnival of the worst passions of human nature'. The introduction of a Highland Games gathering at Stirling in 1870 was widely condemned on the grounds that the nature of the crowds it would attract would have a demoralising effect on the town. Of the Strathallan Games at Bridge of Allan one contemporary noted that 'what began as a means of giving holidays to agricultural workers has become a means of imparting debasing influences ... a periodical pandemonium which is now little better than a drunken orgie (sic)' (Tranter, 1990c: 367). In the course of the late nineteenth and early twentieth centuries the belief that, in practice, an overindulgence in sport had led to moral decline rather than improvement gained increasing support (Lowerson, 1993: 261–97). Whether or not this belief was more representative of contemporary opinion than the more sympathetic attitudes to sport with which it coexisted is difficult to determine. But what can be concluded is that it was sufficiently widespread to cause us to question the validity of the contention that sport was widely supported for the contribution it made to social stability simply by providing an alternative to more demoralising and disruptive activities (Mason, 1989b: 348).

No more convincing is the suggestion that contemporary supporters of sport were extensively motivated by the belief that, through the opportunites it afforded for 'common excitements and shared pleasures', it would work to promote social stability by bridging the gap between the classes. In the sport of soccer an initial mingling of the social classes soon gave way to almost total separation (Mason, 1982: 252, 266). Rowing became increasingly socially segregated as upper middle-class amateur rowers drove 'professional' artisan rowers out of the sport (Halladay: 1987). Angling was a sport in which all classes participated, but rarely within the same space on the river bank or the same institution (Lowerson, 1989b, 15, 26; 1993, 44). Mountaineering and other forms of rock climbing were exclusive to the aristocracy and elite professional classes, while badminton, hockey and lawn tennis remained the preserve of the middle classes until well into the twentieth century (Golby and Purdue, 1984: 181; Lowerson, 1993: 59). Even in cricket, the sport most lauded for its potential for bonding the different social groups, in practice class distinctions were rigidly preserved and perhaps even reinforced (Sandiford, 1994: 80, 165). Control and membership of the MCC and the first-class English county clubs remained the exclusive privilege of the social elites. At humbler levels of the game, in the clubs they joined, in the social composition of the clubs they played against and in the way they played, cricketers were invariably sharply divided on class lines (Williams, 1989: 116–17, 129–30, 138–9). Professionals may often have played in the same teams as amateurs, but always on terms of clearly defined social inferiority and only because, more so than in most other sports, distinctions between the role of the professional and the amateur were

relatively easy to draw and perceive. In this respect cricket resem-
bled the Volunteer Force where, for all the cosmopolitan nature of
its membership, class distinctions were also strictly preserved
(Cunningham, 1980: 124).

A detailed study of the socio-occupational composition of
sportsmen in the Stirling region of Scotland during the second half
of the nineteenth century has confirmed not only that the different
classes generally pursued their own separate sports but also that
participation in the new forms of institutionalised sport by men
from semi-skilled and unskilled occupations, who might be presumed in greatest need of control, was at best modest, at worst
negligible. Roughly nine out of every ten members of the region's
golf clubs were from social class B – annuitants, bank clerks and
other clerical workers, hoteliers and boarding-house keepers,
teachers and farmers, craftsmen or tradesmen employing between
one and twenty-four workers; the rest were from social class A –
the nobility and gentry, men living on private incomes, the larger
employers and high-status professionals like bank managers, doc-
tors and solicitors. Social classes A and B also monopolised the
sports of archery, croquet, foxhunting, lawn tennis, rowing and
rugby and accounted for nearly three-quarters of all club bowlers
and curlers. By contrast, most of the active participants in the
sports of angling, athletics, cricket, quoiting and soccer - nine out
of ten in the cases of athletics, quoiting and soccer and around
two-thirds in the cases of angling and cricket - were drawn from
social classes C (craftsmen and tradesmen employing no labour
other than members of their own family, farmers of less than five
acres, factory and mine workers, policemen, soldiers and the like),
D and E (farm servants, agricultural, general and other labourers,
paupers and similar). The great majority came from social class C.
At least in the early 1880s, the semi-skilled and unskilled workers
of social classes D and E contributed just 22 per cent of all athletes, 16 per cent of all quoiters and soccer players, 13 per cent of
the cricketers, 11 per cent of the anglers, 6 per cent of the curlers,
under 3 per cent of the bowlers and not a single club golfer or tennis player.

Significantly, a soccer match played in 1890 between labourers
from the Carron and Rotterdam Iron Companies was described by
in the press as 'a novel feature of football'. The one reported

instance in the Stirling region when labourers participated in an organised curling match, at Kippen in 1895, was described as 'rather original' and the hope expressed that some of the players might be persuaded to join the local club. For a group which comprised between a quarter and more than a third of the region's total adult male population, men from social classes D and E were obviously heavily underrepresented in institutionalised sport (Tranter, 1987b: 308–11). However much they may have spectated or played casually, even as late as 1914, men from the lowest strata of society took little active part in organised sport and therefore rarely came into direct contact with their social superiors either on the field of play or in the clubhouse (Warren, 1993: 62). Whatever the intention of some of sport's contemporary patrons, the reality is that the Victorian and Edwardian sporting 'revolution' was a phenomenon of class division, not conciliation and, between as well as within individual sports, of widening rather than narrowing division (Bailey, 1978: 129–36, 145; Golby and Purdue, 1984: 156–7, 163, 180–1, 198–200; Clarke and Crichter, 1985: 63, 70; Speak, 1988: 47–9, 58, 61; Lowerson, 1993: 2, 22, 26): as Steve Ickringill so memorably puts it, an excellent example of class exclusiveness 'red in tooth and claw' (Ickringill, 1993: 46).

Fundamental to the creation and persistence of class division in sport was the failure of the reformist minority to persuade the majority of upper- and middle-class men that a regular association with working-class males in sport was a desirable objective. For most of the social elite sport was an opportunity for differentiation not conciliation, and was used to restrict rather than expand contact with social inferiors. In the course of the late nineteenth and early twentieth centuries, as working-class participation in sport grew and the boundaries between the classes became increasingly threatened and as the character of working-class sport was increasingly seen to diverge from the pure 'amateur' ideals of the public school games cult, the desire of the social elite for separatism intensified rather than diminished (Bailey, 1978: 105, 131–46; Cunningham, 1980: 126–9, 132–7; Golby and Purdue, 1984: 182; Clarke and Crichter, 1985: 63).

Arnold Hills, founder of a soccer club at the Thames Ironworks, was by no means the only former public schoolboy and university graduate to withdraw his patronage of working-class sport when it

became clear that its preference for commercialism and professionalism was clashing with his vision of how sport should be practised (Korr, 1978: 219–21). Despite the obvious class
consciousness of the age, open declarations of a preference for
exclusiveness in sport were, of course, rare. But there is no doubt
this existed. The first code of rules for athletics, drawn up by the
Amateur Athletic Club in 1866–7, specifically excluded mechan-
ics, artisans and labourers from participation in an attempt to
divorce amateur athletics from professional pedestrianism and preserve the former exclusively for the upper and middle classes. Even
when the exclusion clause was revoked following the formation of
the Amateur Athletics Association, persistent and successful efforts
continued to be made to distance the sport from professionalism
(Crump, 1989: 51). Golf clubs, it has been argued, were considered ideal vehicles for the display of social status and achievement
by middle-class males anxious to publicise their distinctness from
the labouring masses in a society where class counted for so much
(Lowerson, 1989a: 189). The various sports organisations established by the professional middle classes of Lancaster between the
1840s and 1870s excluded even the most highly paid and
respectable working men from membership (Speak, 1988: 59–60).
Examples like the Airthrey Spa Bowling Club of Bridge of Allan
and the Stirling County Cricket Club suggest that this was often
deliberate. As 'Argus' commented in the *Stirling Observer* of 1885,

no doubt the Stirling County Cricket Club *is* open to anyone. But what
artisan can afford the heavy annual subscription and last season take three
or four trips to Perth, Dundee, Cupar etcetera, thereby losing a day's work
and wages, not to mention the 2s-6d luncheon with which these matches
generally open and the costs of the dress? Artisans may be equal on the
field but they are not made to feel equal in the pavilion ... Little wonder
that Stirling Burgh United and Stirling Wanderers members are reluctant
to play for Stirling County Cricket Club.

The implication that the club was opposed to artisan members
was publicly denied by its secretary and, as if to demonstrate its
openness, the annual subscription was reduced from 21 shillings
for 'ordinary' members to 10s 6d for artisans. Even at this level,
however, it was probably too high for most skilled men, particularly when they could play for clubs like Stirling Burgh United for
as little as 2s 6d a year.

True, there are occasional examples of clubs appearing to make genuine efforts to attract manual workers. In 1883, for instance, the Doune Bowling Club, recognising that its £1 entry fee deterred 'a great number of eligible people from joining', agreed to allow payment to be spread over a year and to charge new members an annual subscription of 1 shilling for each of their first three years instead of the usual 6 shillings. But these were not typical. More typical of the attitude of the more elite, middle-class clubs was the Airthrey Spa Bowling Club, which persisted with an annual subscription of 20 shillings when other bowling clubs in the Stirling region charged between 7s 6d and 12s 6d, and the Stirling Castle Curling Club, which persisted with an annual subscription of 10 shillings and an entry fee of 30 shillings, when less socially prestigious clubs asked for subscriptions of between 1 and 5 shillings and entry fees ranging from zero to 2s 6d or 5 shillings.

In the rigorous definition of amateurism and antipathy to commercialism and professionalism that prevailed in the sports of athletics, cricket, rowing, rugby and soccer, in the split between amateur athletics and pedestrianism, rugby union and rugby league and the middle-class desertion of soccer for rugby, in the servile status accorded to sport's paid employees, in the frequency with which bourgeois organisations failed to promote the cause of working-class sport as well as in the nature of the admission policies typically pursued by predominantly middle-class sports clubs, there are clear indications that for the bulk of the social elite the priority was to keep its sport separate from that of the lower orders. As Tony Mangan concludes, the adoption of the public school games cult by Victorian and Edwardian grammar schools was motivated by a desire on the part of the more humble strata of middle-class society to move closer to their social superiors and further away from their social inferiors. Grammar-school playing fields were seen as symbols of the moral and social superiority of the middle classes over the working classes. Had it been otherwise, we might have expected the state to have made greater efforts than it did to introduce sport rather than drill into the curricula of the elementary schools which provided working-class children with their education (Mangan, 1983: 313, 329–30).

The general conclusion must be that in intention as well as in practice the effect of the sporting 'revolution' was to sharpen not blur the boundaries between the middle and working classes (Holt, 1989: 107–17, 347–8; Mason, 1989a: 346; Lowerson, 1993: 21–2). In the opinion of its most recent historian, cricket failed to bridge the gap between the classes precisely because most of its elite and bourgeois supporters never intended it to (Sandiford, 1994: 162, 170). If sport *was* perceived as a vehicle for social stability, outside a minority of reformers it was not intended to achieve this objective through the integration of working-class men into the sports and sporting institutions of their social superiors.

To some of its contemporary elite patrons, however, sport served to foster social stability not so much by providing the working classes with an alternative to crime and drink or a greater opportunity to mingle with their social betters but, more subtly, by persuading them to adopt the forms and ideologies of sport recently accepted by the bourgeoisie (Bailey, 1978: 91, 94, 128–9; Holt, 1989: 136). For historians who continue to emphasise the significance of social control motives for the Victorian and Edwardian sporting 'revolution' this interpretation is especially attractive. According to this theory, organised, codified forms of sport, with their stress on fair play and respect for rules, playing for the team rather than for self, participation rather than winning at all costs and amateurism rather than professionalism, were first introduced in elite public schools during the 1830s and 1840s as a means of disciplining unruly pupils and increasing the attractiveness of the school to the rising urban bourgeoisie. By the 1860s the playing of inter-school games had helped to create a cohesiveness in the public school sector which was shortly to be formalised in the Headmasters' Conference of 1869. Once established in the public schools, the games cult, and the virtues of self-restraint, selflessness, decency and responsibility which supposedly flowed from it, was taken to the working classes by proselytisers who believed that it would prove an equally effective force for discipline in society as a whole (Dunning, 1975: 117, 119–36; Dunning and Sheard, 1979: 65–99, 139–40; Mangan: 1981).

The thesis is presented in its most sophisticated form by John Hargreaves. Between the 1780s and the 1840s, Hargreaves argues, society's dominant groups had attempted to control the labouring populations primarily by force, using the agencies of law and order to outlaw traditional sporting pastimes whose brutality and disorderliness were perceived as particularly threatening to social stability. Over the course of the second half of the nineteenth century, partly because the effectiveness of this strategy was steadily eroded by a lack of unity among the dominant groups themselves, the crudity of force gave way to a more subtle, persuasive approach which, by encouraging the working classes to copy bourgeois ways and mentalities of sport, aimed either to persuade *all* subordinates to adopt the behavioural norms of their superiors or, more subtly still, to spread these norms only to skilled workers. This reinforced the divisions between the skilled and articulate, on the one hand, and the semi-skilled, unskilled and inarticulate, on the other, and thus minimised the potential for effective, mass opposition to the established order. As the process of political democratisation accelerated in the later decades of the century, Hargreaves claims, the need to employ hegemonic rather than openly repressive measures to exact deference and demonstrate authority intensified (Hargreaves, 1985: 219–20, 225–6; 1986a: 246–7, 250–3; 1986b: 26–86).

Powerfully argued though this thesis is, it has often been pointed out that the assumptions on which it rests are backed up by surprisingly little empirical evidence (Reiss, 1994: 4). To assume, for instance, that society's dominant groups were united in their support for the public-school games' ideology ignores the fact that, in reality, no such unity existed (Bailey, 1989: 114; Mason, 1989a: 347–8). Even in the elite public schools, where a minority of self-styled 'socratic teachers' strenuously defended the interests of cultural and intellectual education against the emphasis of the majority on the priority of sport, support for the games cult and its supposed hegemonic function was far from unanimous (Dewey, 1995: 51–2). Outside the public schools, unanimity was still less evident. In their more sympathetic attitudes to professionalism and distinctly non-public school preference for playing to win, the commercial and manufacturing elites of the north and Midlands took a very different view of the meaning and purpose of sport from that of the ex-public school and university alumni of the south of England and east of Scotland professional classes (Mason, 1982: 265; Holt, 1989: 349–50, 364; Williams, 1989: 313).

Much of the more recent research suggests that, inside as well as outside the public schools in which it first emerged and was nurtured, a belief in the socially stabilising powers of bourgeois forms of sport was less widespread than hegemony theory requires. The fact that the creation of an 'amateur' games cult at schools like Shrewsbury and Westminster owed as much to the initiative of pupils as to the imposition of headmasters itself implies that the motives which underlay it were considerably more complex than a simple desire on the part of school authorities for higher standards of discipline (Chandler, 1988b: 312–13). In the world beyond the public schools and universities the failure to establish team games in elementary schools, the modest contribution of employers to the growth of works' teams and company physical recreation programmes, the reluctance of local government, the churches, colliery owners and landowners to assist in the provision of sport facilities for Northumberland miners and the fact that clubs in working-class sports like soccer drew their directors not from the ranks of big business and the professional classes but from the local petty bourgeoisie – who were least likely to share the values of the public-school games' cult – all lead to the conclusion that only a minority of the dominant groups in society believed in the stabilising power of sport. Despite the best efforts of a handful of reformers to persuade it otherwise, the bulk of elite opinion was more inclined to believe that the team-based games which were central to the public-school games' ideology were legitimate only for meeting the character-building requirements of society's leaders and not for the training of those who were to be led, and that what manual workers most needed were mental rather than physical forms of recreation (Bailey, 1978: 98, 130–1; Hay, 1982: 241; Golby and Purdue, 1984: 168; Holt, 1989: 143, 152, 164).

Such limited faith in the hegemonic powers of sport as there was among the social elite was almost certainly further eroded by the way in which working-class sport evolved in the course of the later Victorian and Edwardian periods. Historians continue to dispute the scale and causation of player and spectator misconduct in working-class sport, particularly in soccer, the sport most prone to disorder. Inter-club Welsh rugby matches, it has been claimed, were frequently marred by violence among spectators and grounds often closed by the game's authorities as punishment for crowd disturbances (Williams, 1988: 131–2). According to Hutchinson, 'riots, unruly behaviour, violence, assault and vandalism were a well-established ... pattern of crowd behaviour at football matches during the late 1870s and 1880s, though their frequency declined from the 1890s' (Hutchinson: 1975). Utilising data on ground closures and club cautions recorded in the minute books of the English FA for the years 1895–7 and 1910–12, Vamplew argues that the incidence of soccer crowd disturbance did not begin to decline until the 1900s, an improvement he attributes principally to stricter policing and the growing practice of segregating rival fans. Like Hutchinson, however, Vamplew believes that as late as 1914 the problem of soccer crowd misbehaviour was far from negligible. Data on the number of cautions for spectator misconduct issued to clubs by the Scottish FA, indeed, appear to suggest that in Scotland the problem actually increased (Vamplew, 1980: 6–7, 15–17; 1988b: 271–5, 363–4). Between 1894 and 1914 the *Leicester Daily Mercury* reported 159 separate incidents of crowd disorder in the Leicestershire area alone. Assuming that similar levels of disorder occurred elsewhere, this implies a total of over 4,000 outbreaks of soccer crowd misconduct in England as a whole. Contrary to the conclusion suggested by the data extracted from the minute books of the English FA, moreover, the Leicestershire newspaper evidence shows no decline in levels of disorder, the annual average number of recorded incidents falling from 7.6 between 1894 and 1900 to 6.7 between 1901 and 1907 but then rising to 8.4 between 1908 and 1914 (Dunning *et al.*, 1984: 222–5, 229).

Other historians take a different view. From evidence contained in the records of the Birmingham FA it has been claimed that levels of spectator misconduct between 1880 and 1914 were low compared with those of the 1960s to early 1980s and that pre-1914 soccer crowds were generally well behaved and never considered a serious threat to public order (Mason, 1980: 166–7; Crump and Mason: 1985). In the Stirling region of Scotland crowd troubles were reported no more frequently than at one in every 200 matches involving soccer clubs of senior status (Tranter, 1995: 130). In Lancashire between 1884 and 1914 they were equally rare (Lewis, 1996: 319). Although more research is needed to confirm the point, on balance it seems likely that, relative to the number of games played and the number of spectators they attracted, incidents of crowd misconduct in soccer were atypical and rarely serious enough to pose a real threat to social stability. Frustration disorders, caused by dissatisfaction over access to a game or the way it was played or adjudicated, were by far the most common triggers of disturbance before 1914, and few of these were prolonged or especially severe. Only when disturbances were provoked by conflict between rival ethnic or religious groups (confrontational disorders) or by particularly intense outbursts of emotion aroused by victory or defeat (expressive disorders), as at Cappielow in 1899 and Hampden Park in 1909, did they reach levels that were genuinely threatening to social stability. Fortunately, outbreaks of this kind were infrequent. Rarer still were disturbances triggered by political grievances (remonstrance disorders) or by the activities of minorities using soccer as a convenient vehicle for satisfying their desire for anti-social behaviour (Vamplew, 1988b: 267–8, 270; Mason, 1989b: 172–4; Tranter, 1995: 130–6; Lewis, 1996: 323, 326, 332).

Almost certainly, even in soccer where they were most frequent, instances of working-class spectator misconduct at sporting events were sufficiently uncommon for us to agree with Allen Guttmann that at least one requirement of the public-school games' cult – the ability of spectators to behave with decency and restraint – was the norm among working-class sports crowds long before 1914 (Guttmann, 1969: 123). At the same time, it is important to stress that this view would not have been shared by the majority of contemporaries. Whatever the reality, by the 1880s and 1890s most middle-class observers were convinced that working-class sports like soccer were not only prone to unacceptably high levels of violence, hooliganism and poor sportsmanship among their players and spectators but also, in their commitment to commercialism, professionalism and victory at almost any cost, were being watched and played in a manner that bore little resemblance to their own preferred 'amateur' ideal. Long before the end of the nineteenth century the bulk of elite opinion either had little interest in working-class sport or had come to regard it with positive distaste. As a result, except among a rump of the most zealous reformers, any ambition the social elites may once have harboured of achieving social stability by encouraging even the more 'respectable' sections of working-class society to adopt bourgeois values and practices in sport must long since have been extinguished (Bailey, 1978: 145; Thompson, 1981: 201; Mason, 1982: 254–5, 257, 262–4; Golby and Purdue, 1984: 167, 182; Holt, 1989: 144–5, 151).

Perhaps the greatest single weakness in the hegemonic interpretation of the Victorian and Edwardian sporting 'revolution' is its tendency to understate the ability of working-class culture to resist the attempted imposition of elite ideologies and determine its own behavioural norms. At its most sophisticated, even the hegemonic thesis accepts that working-class culture was powerful enough to ensure that attempts to impose middle-class norms on the sports of the masses would never be completely successful (Bailey, 1989: 113; Holt, 1989: 363–4; Mason, 1989a: 346). To critics of the thesis this admission fails to take adequate account of the magnitude of the divergence between middle- and working-class sporting cultures (Birley, 1995: 31–67). In their definitions of the concept of 'manliness', for example, the two cultures remained fundamentally opposed. To the middle classes 'manliness' in sport meant amateurism, self-restraint, strict obedience to rules and active participation rather than passive spectating: to the working classes it meant professionalism, a greater emphasis on physical aggression, commitment to spectatorism as much as to playing and a willingness wherever possible to subvert the rules in the interests of winning (Maguire: 1986).

As illustrated by the survival of traditional sports among the miners of Northumberland and the transformation of rugby in west Yorkshire from an amateur to a professional sport following an influx of working-class players and spectators in the 1880s (Metcalfe, 1990: 361; Collins, 1995: 33, 36, 39–40, 42, 47), whenever the two ideologies came into conflict it was often the working-class version which proved the stronger. In practice, it is argued, the ability of working-class sport to avoid wholesale submission to bourgeois values and fashion its own sporting style was far greater than Hargreaves allows. Invariably, middle-class practices were adopted only when they suited working-class preferences and could be incorporated, with amendments where necessary, into working-class cultural norms which in many of their essentials remained much the same as they had always been. The role of the social elites in promoting the new forms of organised, codified sport among the labouring masses, the critics of the hegemonic interpretation claim, was predominantly one of 'sponsor not missionary', supplying much valuable, practical assistance but little of the ideology of sport favoured by the bourgeoisie (Cunningham,

1980: 128; Thompson, 1981: 189–90, 201, 207–8; Hay, 1982: 228; Golby and Purdue, 1984: 100, 116, 167; Holt, 1989: 135, 153, 165, 363–5).

Few historians would deny that a concern for stability on the part of society's elites made some contribution to the spread of organised, codified forms of sport among the working classes of late Victorian and Edwardian Britain. Most, however, would prefer not to overstate its role. As Ickringill shows in his explanation for the more widespread and successful opposition to commercialism and professionalism in sport in Britain than in the USA (1993), elite attitudes and actions were often as likely to impede as to facilitate the diffusion of sport. To see the 'revolution' in sport as *chiefly* the consequence of a search for social harmony is also to ignore a number of other awkward facts.

One of these is the fact that many of the middle-class men most closely involved in the promotion of working-class sport had little contact with the public-school games' ideology and little sympathy with the behavioural values it sought to inculcate. A second is that, compared with the numbers whose characters and behaviour were moulded by the principal institutions of socialisation – the family, the workplace, education and the state – the numbers of working-class males regularly playing or even watching the type of sports redolent with the spirit of the 'pure' public school games' ethic was surely too small to convince at least the more perceptive of contemporary observers that sport could be a significant stabilising influence (Hay, 1982: 227–9, 233–4, 237–8, 241–2). To the extent that an elite faith in the ability of sport to foster social stability did exist, it was in any case steadily eroded by the evident failure of the different classes to come together in sport and of much of working-class society to adopt bourgeois norms of spectating and play.

A third is the existence of a greater capacity on the part of working-class sport for determining its own forms and modes of conduct than it is safe to permit in the social control interpretation. Above all, perhaps, an explanation for the 'revolution' in sport based too exclusively around the concern for social stability oversimplifies the causes of a complex phenomenon. In their efforts to explain the working-class preference for rugby union in south Wales and rugby league and soccer in northern England, the replacement of rugby by soccer in the West Riding of Yorkshire and the diffusion of amateur boxing from the middle classes to the working classes, most historians tend to give priority to factors other than an attempt on the part of the elites to impose sport in the interests of social control (Russell: 1988; Holt, 1989: 153; Shipley, 1989: 90). These factors will be considered in the next chapter.

5

For health, prestige or profit?

Whatever the precise mechanism through which it was intended to work, the promotion of organised, codified forms of sport as a force for social control was by no means the only nor, arguably, even the the most important motive underlying the Victorian and Edwardian sporting 'revolution'. Trawling the legacy of contemporary comment and historical analysis, indeed, yields almost as many motives for participation and patronage as there were sports to indulge in, each varying markedly in the significance of its impact by time, place, social class and sport and from individual to individual according to age, sex, personal inclination or circumstance.

Perhaps because it served no grand utilitarian purpose, one of the most frequently stated reasons for participating in sport, the sheer enjoyment it provided, was largely overlooked by earlier historians. Yet, as more recent research has shown, for many people in all social classes sport was attractive simply for the pleasure it brought. To John MacFarlane, founder and patron of the first Stirling Boat Club, it was quite sufficient that the only benefit of boat-racing for spectators was the 'excitement and enjoyment' it generated. To R. J. Girdwood, their secretary, the Strathallan Highland Games were valued 'as much for the enjoyment they provide for residents as for their power in attracting visitors'. For the working men who formed the crew of the Scottish Central Rowing Club in the 1850s 'the only object (was) amusement after working hours'. The Borestone Bowling Club, founded in 1858, and the Callander Highland Games, begun in 1888, are just two of many examples of sporting organisations in the Stirling region of Scotland inaugurated 'solely to provide amusement' (Tranter, 1989a: 243). As Dr E. S. Morley, chairman of the Blackburn Rovers

Football Club, put it when asked to explain why middle-class men watched soccer, 'the fact was somewhat after that given by the old lady when asked why she had a drop of gin and water at night ... some folks takes it 'cause it does em good; but I takes it 'cause I likes it' (Mason, 1982: 253). According to Cunningham, working-class men joined the Volunteer Force neither to demonstrate their patriotism and manliness nor from a desire to associate more closely with their social superiors but simply to take advantage of the recreational facilities it offered (Cunningham, 1980: 126). A straightforward pursuit of pleasure figured extensively in the motives of many middle-class anglers and, to judge from the heavy financial losses they were willing to incur, in the motives of many of those who participated in horseracing, hunting, shooting and yachting (Vamplew, 1976: 178–85; 1988b: 107; 1989, 227; Huggins, 1987: 110; Lowerson, 1989b: 24–5). Even cricket, the sport most often endowed with aims of a more elevated nature, is not immune from the possibility that many of its followers participated chiefly for the pleasure it brought. Thus, while one historian argues that the Georgians played cricket for enjoyment and the Victorians for spiritual and moral regeneration (Sandiford, 1994: 2), another suggests that enjoyment remained one of the principal reasons for involvement throughout the Victorian and Edwardian periods (Williams, 1989: 130).

What it was that made sport such an enjoyable experience and why it was that in Victorian and Edwardian Britain so many more people than ever before reached out to it for their enjoyment remain matters of dispute. All historians would agree that the capacity of sport to generate pleasure had much to do with the opportunity it afforded to indulge man's passion for gambling. Certainly, in sports as diverse as boatracing, coarse fishing, horseracing, pedestrianism, quoiting and, by the end of the Victorian era, soccer, gambling was widespread. Of all the major participant and spectator sports, only in cricket did the Georgian enthusiasm for gambling largely disappear in the second half of the nineteenth century (Sandiford, 1994: 21, 80). For some historians one of the other principal attractions of sport was the opportunity it provided for satisfying man's emotional need for camaraderie and companionship, a need that was given fresh impetus by his diminishing role in the affairs of the family and household and the increasingly individualistic and competitive nature of the public world of work (Holt, 1989: 153, 155, 173; Lowerson, 1989a: 189; 1993: 18; Williams, 1989: 130).

Sometimes, however, these same and other historians take the completely opposite view and see sport as an escape from the stifling cooperativeness demanded by home and workplace into a world where man's natural craving for competition, personal glory and a measure of independence and isolation could be more easily satisfied (Mason, 1982: 262; Metcalfe, 1982: 474; Lowerson, 1989a: 189; 1989b, 14; Holt, 1989: 164–5; Reiss, 1994: 154, 173; Sandiford, 1994: 168).

To yet other historians sport was enjoyable chiefly because it improved the quality of life among a population starved of adequate opportunities for recreation and struggling to come to terms with what was for some the boredom and for others the excessive strain of urban industrial life. 'How pleasant and encouraging to see gentlemen desirous of promoting our pastimes and breaking that monotony of which so many people complain', the *Bridge of Allan Reporter* commented on the gift of a pair of silver-mounted bowls to the Wellhouse Bowling Club in 1866. 'Let Bridge of Allan and Stirling have its one night of freedom from the restraints our refined civilisation has imposed on its citizens' the *Stirling Journal* wrote in 1890 in defence of the Friday evening shows which preceded the Strathallan Highland Games. Sports like cricket and horseracing were widely valued for providing an essential break from 'the tedium of factory and mine' and 'the dull and wearying round of daily work' (Huggins, 1987: 100; Tranter, 1989a: 241–2, 247; Sandiford, 1994: 55).

Of course, the rhetoric of sport was based on much more than merely the potential it afforded for enjoyment. In an age when the pursuit of pleasure for its own sake often provoked powerful feelings of guilt, those who preached the virtues of sport also felt it necessary to imbue it with a capacity for fulfilling a number of crucial, practical functions. One of the most important of these, it has been suggested, was the contribution it made to the creation of a sense of community identity. Among the social elites of both Britain and its colonies there was a widespread assumption that sport would play a vital role in establishing and maintaining the unity of the Empire and Commonwealth. On the whole, historians have tended to agree that this assumption was matched by reality. In the short term cricket tours to and from the colonies did help bond the Empire together, exactly as they were intended to (Sandiford, 1994: 42, 155-7, 166). In the longer term, through the impact of colonial sporting success on the colonies' own sense of identity and self-esteem and on Britain's willingness to treat them as independent equals, Anglo-colonial competition in sport helped smooth the eventual transition from Empire to Commonwealth (Perkin, 1989: 145; Holt, 1989: 203-8, 212, 219, 221-3).

As Tony Mangan has recently emphasised, sport was also widely and successfully promoted as a force for national cohesion in reponse to the growth of 'tribal nationalism' elsewhere (Mangan, 1995, 8-9). The revival of Highland Games gatherings in Victorian Scotland, it has been argued, owed much to a desire to raise levels of national consciousness (Jarvie, 1991: 43, 67):

Never was there a time when the ancient renown of Scotland needed to be more celebrated and maintained. Many great landowners by turning their estates into extensive farms have caused thousands of Highlanders to emigrate. Unless something is done to revive the popular spirit of the Highlands, its games and exercises, the sound of the Gaelic language and the pibroch will soon disppear from the northern glens,

the *Stirling Observer* commented when announcing the date of the Stirling Highland Games gathering in 1855.

In Wales, as well as working to reinforce local, internal community identities and rivalries, rugby, more so than politics or religion, was helping to create a powerful, if highly masculinised, sense of nationhood among the disparate immigrant groups that made up its population (Williams, 1988: 131, 141; Holt, 1989: 237, 250; Andrews: 1996). The extraordinary popularity of soccer in late nineteenth- and early twentieth-century Scotland likewise owed a good deal to the part it played in strengthening nationalist sentiment and unity in the face of England's economic supremacy and cultural invasiveness (Moorhouse: 1987; Holt, 1989: 237, 253, 258). Within each nation, while matches between soccer clubs representing different parts of the same community often exacerbated divisions, at the level of the community they represented soccer clubs were powerful agents of communal identity and solidarity. For working-class males, especially, sports like soccer were critical to the establishment of an identity with place at a time when the increasing scale of urbanisation and the trend towards nationwide competitive structures had all but destroyed the comforting sense of belonging that had existed in the smaller communities and more localised geography of experience of earlier ages (Mason, 1982: 257–60, 265; Golby and Purdue, 1984: 167; Metcalfe, 1988: 285, 287; Holt, 1989: 166–9, 172–3, 363).

To some historians a no less significant motive for contemporary participation in sport was the contribution it was expected to make to individual or community status and prestige. For working-class men success in sport or the ownership of a few shares in the local soccer club provided an opportunity for social advance or, more realistically, for gaining or sharing in the status and respect accorded to the sporting champion and his associates (Holt, 1989: 285; Mason, 1989b: 165; Sandiford, 1994: 167). For upper- and middle-class patrons and participants sport was often a means of either flaunting social status or enhancing popularity and reputation and, in some cases, even of securing electoral support (Malcolmson, 1973: 66, 85; Bailey, 1978: 143; Mason, 1982: 265). For those of the elite classes who invested in the ownership of race horses and for the businessmen who became directors and shareholders in English and, particularly, Scottish soccer clubs, it seems, the search for prestige dominated all other motives (Vamplew, 1976: 183; 1988b, 157, 172–3; 1989, 227–8; Holt, 1989: 284–5; Mason, 1989b: 164–5).

As a cause of the Victorian and Edwardian sporting 'revolution', a desire to enhance the prestige of the community mattered just as much as the concern for individual status. Among the members of English county cricket clubs priority was given not to maximising returns on their investment but to ensuring the survival of the club as a service to the community (Vamplew, 1988b: 98, 110; Sandiford, 1994: 63, 71). As expressed by Sir Thomas Martineau, a director of the Edgbaston Cricket Ground Company, the main purpose of those who bought shares should be 'not to make dividends but to advance the interests and position of the county club' (Sandiford and Vamplew, 1986: 320–1).

At the other end of the social ladder the popularity of soccer among the working classes also owed something to the opportunity it gave for demonstrating pride in community (Metcalfe, 1982: 486, 492, 494; Holt, 1988: 77; 1989: 166). So, too, did the growing willingness of municipal authorities and elites to invest in the provision of decent sports facilities. It was solely to prevent the city from 'falling behind places of lesser size and population' that the leading citizens of Dunblane in 1880 were urged to contribute to the cost of opening a games park. 'Boatracing is now a favourite amusement even at obscure, remote places and we don't see why Stirling should be behind its neighbours in this respect', the *Stirling Journal* remarked in 1853. 'If Alva and Tillicoultry can have them surely Alloa can?', the *Alloa Advertiser* complained two years later about the lack of a Highland Games gathering in the town. Once established, sporting organisations were expected to represent the community with credit and were fiercely criticised when they did not. 'It is little short of a disgrace to the club that they allow the cup to leave the town every year ... surely there are as many gentlemen amateurs as might form a crew which could maintain the credit of our ancient town against allcomers?', the *Stirling Journal* wrote in 1858 of the persistent failure of the Stirling Boat Club to win the premier trophy at its own regatta (Tranter, 1989a: 242, 244).

For most historians, however, the utilitarian objectives which come closest to rivalling a concern for social stability as the principal motivators of the sporting revolution are the contributions sport was assumed to make to health and profit.

By the third quarter of the nineteenth century an active participation in sport was widely regarded as an essential requirement for the high standards of physical, mental and moral well-being which it was thought Christian man owed a duty to his Creator to attain (Mangan, 1981: 33, 39, 46, 50, 53; 1988: 90, 98; Lowerson, 1989a: 188; 1993, 17–18, 42, 89, 127; Reiss, 1994: 150, 154, 173). 'Of all athletic games, none offers so fine a scope as quoiting for bringing into full prominence the qualities of body and eye', claimed Alexander Blackwood, chairman of the Milngavie Craigton Quoits Club in 1898 (Tranter, 1990a: 52). Golf 'fostered health in body and mind'. Highland games were 'good for the nerves'. Football combatted the 'sedentary occupations, excessive reading and close application to business' of the 'clerk, teacher and artisan' and provided 'vital mental stimulus for young men shut up in factories, warehouses and shops'. Bowling was 'as favourable to mental ease as to physical well-being'. Cricket 'exercised the physical and mental energies of our young men' (Tranter, 1989a: 239-40). A healthy body, it was assumed, was the *sine qua non* of an alert, perceptive mind and of the type of moral character which would reject sexual deviance, promiscuity and effeminacy in favour of purity, manliness and the virtues of stoicism, pluck, self-reliance, and an unshakeable commitment to fair dealing (Holt, 1989: 88–94, 97; Lowerson, 1993: 19; Sandiford, 1994: 35, 42).

In part, the growing concern for health was prompted simply by what were perceived to be the damaging consequences of urban industrialisation for standards of human physical and mental welfare. Sport was seen as a necessary antidote both to the problems of poor physical health caused by the squalor of urban environments and to the greater mental exertion required by a more sophisticated and competitive commercial and industrial world (Holt, 1989: 88; Lowerson, 1989a: 188).

But the promotion of health through sport was also expected to have two additional benefits. The first was the contribution it would make to the availability of men with the physical and mental qualities necessary for success on the battlefield and for governing the Empire (Bailey, 1978: 125–6; Birley, 1995: 154–70; Chandler: 1996; Mangan: 1996; Martens: 1996). In 1895, for example, a Sheffield sports paper quoted with approval the view of 'an eminent German military authority' that football 'renders conscription unnecessary because, though it does not make trained soldiers of our young men, it enhances in them the spirit of pluck, opposition, competition, never-know-when-they-are beaten, never-say die ... kind of feeling which tends to the greatness of our national character' (Mason, 1982: 250). As late as the outbreak of the First World War an officer of the British Expeditionary Force to France still felt able to claim that 'the individual superiority of the Briton over the Hun is due to our natural love for sports'. Even at the end of the war there were many who continued to believe that victory had been the result of the nation's commitment to sport (Lowerson, 1993: 292, 294).

The second anticipated benefit of the positive effect of sport on health was the improvement it was expected to generate in the productivity of the workforce. Some employers set up works' teams in the hope that increases in output would follow the psychological boost of victory (Mason, 1982: 266). Others, like Arnold Hills, believed that sport raised productivity primarily by improving relations between management and men or attracting a better quality of worker (Korr, 1978: 216, 219). But for the majority of those who patronised working-class sport in the interests of labour productivity it was the impact of sport on physical rather than mental health that mattered most. By the second half of the nineteenth century, in contrast to an earlier consensus which regarded time spent in leisure as time wasted, employers generally had come to accept that sport was a positive complement to work, reinvigorating rather than debilitating and thus conducive to an increase rather than a decrease in the efficiency of labour (Myerscough, 1974: 8, 12; Bailey, 1978: 81; Cunningham, 1980: 198). Employers like George Cadbury had no doubt that, by reducing the extent of labour turnover and the risk of industrial injury and improving the facility for 'quick, well-executed work ... manual dexterity and visual awareness', regular participation in sport raised the productivity of their workers (Holt, 1989: 143, 150–1; Reiss, 1994: 164). Many would have agreed with the claim made by James Kerr, a vice-president of the English FA, that among the 2,500 young men belonging to clubs affiliated to the Lancashire FA was 'a capacity to do a higher average work than among any other 2,500 young men in Lancashire' (Mason, 1982: 250–1). Augmented by growing anxiety over the rise of foreign industrial and political competition and the Darwinian belief that only the fittest could expect to survive, it is not surprising that 'physical education' was extensively advocated as vital for ensuring that 'healthy constitution which is so much needed in this age of progress and activity' (Bailey, 1978: 127; Tranter, 1989a: 240).

Considerations of labour productivity, however, affected only a small proportion of those who were attracted to sport in the hope of making money. For the great majority the essential commercial attraction of sport was the opportunity it offered for paid employment or a profitable return to investment. At least some of the working-class males who took up sports such as boxing, cricket and soccer must have been encouraged to do so by the possibility that it might lead to a professional career and the higher material standard of life that, rightly or wrongly, was assumed to come with it (Mason, 1982, 262; Sandiford, 1994, 166). Sports like angling, crown green bowling, pedestrianism and quoiting provided leading players with an opportunity to earn substantial sums from exhibition, tournament and head-to-head, stake-money matches. The chance to compete for stakes of between £50 and £200 a side at major quoiting matches must have been a powerful attraction to working-class men. At a time when skilled workers rarely earned more than £1–2 a week, even stakes of between £5 and £25 a side wagered at the more typical quoiting contest would have been reason enough for men to consider taking up the sport (Lowerson, 1989b: 28; Tranter, 1990a: 51, 56, 63).

Whether expectations of personal financial gain were as influential a reason for involvement among those who preferred to invest rather than actively participate in sport is more difficult to determine. Even in the case of soccer, where they were most common, the per capita number of shares owned by working-class investors was far too small to permit the conclusion that the pursuit of profit was the main reason for investment. Among middle-class investors, on the other hand, the opportunities sport provided for making money were a more important motive. From the frequency with which they established clubs and competitions in the sport of angling and supplied trophies and prize money for horserace meetings, bowling, curling and quoiting clubs, Highland Games gatherings and pigeon-shooting contests, it is clear that the hoteliers, innkeepers and publicans of Victorian and Edwardian Britain were as interested in promoting sport for personal material gain as their predecessors had been (Huggins, 1987: 103, 115; Lowerson, 1988: 120–1; 1989b: 19, 27; Tranter: 1989a). As Tony Mason notes, while some middle-class patrons sponsored sport in an attempt to keep working men out of the pub, others did so to draw them into it (Mason, 1982: 265). For publicans like John Houlding, founder of the Liverpool Football Club, the cycle manufacturers who sponsored meetings and riders in order to advertise their products, the shopkeepers for whom sports crowds were good for business, the residential developers who built golf courses in order to attract investors, raise house prices and facilitate sales, the directors and shareholders of cycling, horseracing and indoor bowling companies, bookmakers and boxing promoters, most owners of race horses and bloodstock breeders and those who invested in soccer clubs in the hope of securing a building, catering or outfitting contract, a desire to make money out of sport was clearly an important, perhaps even the most important, motive for participation (Vamplew, 1982: 557, 567; 1988b: 100–1, 110, 179–80; Mason, 1982: 265; Lowerson, 1993: 242–3).

At the same time, the significance of personal profit maximisation as a motive for investment in sport should not be overstated. To suggest that the growth of sports like professional soccer stemmed primarily from the concern of investors for profit is to go too far. To judge from the evidence of admission charges, player wage and transfer practices, the method of allocating gate receipts between clubs, the number and type of fixtures played, the infrequent use of stadia for non-footballing activities, the rarity with which dividends were paid to shareholders even by clubs that could afford to pay them and the general absence of policies designed to equalise competition between clubs, neither the Scottish Football League nor any of its member clubs appear to have given priority to maximising the profits of investors. The fact that few shareholders ever complained about the failure of their investment to yield a return seems to confirm that, for the majority, the chief reason for investing was other than financial gain.

In the case of the (English) Football League, where greater efforts were made to prevent competition from other leagues, restrict costs and equalise the playing strength of the different clubs by limiting signing-on bonuses (in 1891) and introducing a maximum wage (in 1901), the interest of shareholders in making money from their investment was more obvious. In part the difference reflected the higher proportion of working-class shareholders in Scottish than English soccer clubs. This circumstance also helps to explain why profit-maximising objectives were less evident in soccer as a whole than in sports like angling and horseracing and among investors in ice-rink, indoor bowling and general recreation companies where the cost of invidual shares was usually higher, the average number of shares held by each shareholder larger and the proportion of middle-class shareholders greater. In part the difference was a consequence of differences in the type of middle-class shareholder involved. In Scotland soccer club shareholders included an unusually high percentage of men from the drinks trades whose commercial interests were better served by the large crowds generated by a winning team and housed in an extensive stadium than by the direct returns on their shares. In England shareholders were more often drawn from businessmen who were less likely to benefit from the sale of a product to the crowd and therefore more inclined to seek their profit from the shares they held. Yet even in England the main aim of most soccer club directors and shareholders was to win matches, not maximise returns to their investment. While most soccer club prospectuses emphasised the benefits local businessmen could expect from the expenditures of spectators attracted to matches, very few promised to pay dividends to investors.

By inhibiting the free movement of players and thus helping to equalise standards of play between clubs, the adoption of maximum wage and retain and transfer policies to some extent may have been designed to facilitate profit maximisation. On the other hand, the fact that dividends were more often than not never paid and restricted by law to a maximum of 5 per cent when they were, the persistence of admission charges that were standard to most clubs in the same competition, the willingness to play so many unremunerative matches and the general reluctance to raise revenue by using grounds for non-footballing purposes, all suggest that, in England as in Scotland, the bulk of directors and shareholders did not intend, or expect, their investment to yield a direct return. Even the possibility of indirect returns from the sale of alcohol or building, catering and equipment contracts was probably a significant motive for investment for only a minority of those who bought shares (Mason, 1980, 49; Vamplew, 1982: 552, 554–7, 559, 561, 563-7; 1988b: 77–87, 110, 152, 157–8, 170, 172, 176; Holt, 1989: 284–5).

A similar conclusion holds for the great majority of those who invested in rugby league and cricket. In neither sport were the controlling bodies primarily concerned with maximising the profits of their members or member clubs. Except perhaps during its earliest years, the Northern Rugby Football Union made no attempt to ensure that equality of playing strength between clubs which is so essential to the achievement of profit maximisation. Nor did the MCC, the controlling body of English first-class cricket, which insisted on residential qualifications and non-transferable benefits for its players, rejected the idea of a two-divisional county championship incorporating promotion and relegation and steadfastly refused to subsidise the poorer county clubs. From the nature of the wage policies they implemented, the number of matches they sanctioned, their failure to make first-class cricket more appealing to working-class spectators and their refusal to adopt company status or do much to raise revenue from non-cricketing activities, it is clear that personal profit maximisation was also of little interest to the majority of those who paid to become members of county clubs. Where profits were made, they were used to improve facilities and strengthen the playing staff rather than to line members' pockets (Sandiford and Vamplew, 1986: 311, 313–21; Vamplew, 1988b: 87–95, 98, 110, 116, 119, 121, 123, 152–3; Holt, 1989: 286–7; Sandiford, 1994: 63).

Owners and breeders of race horses and shareholders in racecourse companies showed a greater interest in profit maximisation. Probably a majority of owners and breeders hoped to make money and shareholders certainly expected to receive a dividend. In the considerable efforts that were made to attract working-class spectators and to make horseracing more exciting and appealing to gamblers by introducing sprints, handicaps and races for two-year old horses, the marketing policies and race programmes of racecourse companies show at least some concern for maximising profits. But not all owners and breeders were profit maximisers and the sport's governing body, the Jockey Club, was more interested in ensuring the survival of horseracing than in bolstering the profits of investors. The fact that most of the shareholders in racecourse companies were content with the moderate, maximum rates of return allowed by Jockey Club rules and happily invested in racecourses like Stockton, which opened just three days a year, suggests that even in horseracing many investors were motivated by much more than a simple desire for the largest possible financial return (Vamplew, 1976: 42; 1988b, 110, 113–14, 179, 217–18; Huggins, 1987: 109).

To some extent, at least, the income-generating potential of investment in sport also acted as an inducement to institutional and community involvement. From brass bands and boys' brigades to bands of hope, public park committees, oddfellows' and foresters' associations and temperance societies, the promotion of sporting events – amateur athletics meetings, cycle races, quoiting and five-a-side soccer tournaments in particular – was widely seen as a way of raising funds (Tranter, 1989a: 244–5). Transport companies sponsored horseraces in order to profit from the increase in passenger traffic that would result (Vamplew, 1988b: 180). The *Hull Times* underwrote the cost of fishing matches and, in common with other newspapers, provided sport with free publicity in the hope of boosting sales (Lowerson, 1988: 121; Vamplew, 1988b: 180). Seaside resorts like Blackpool and Bournemouth invested in golf courses, bowling greens and sea-fishing competitions as much for the revenue that would accrue from the residents and visitors they would attract as for their contribution to civic standing (Lowerson, 1989a: 192; 1989b: 32; 1993: 134). Municipal corporations on Tees-side donated trophies and prize money to horserace meetings in order to draw the crowds that would benefit local tradesmen (Huggins, 1987: 103). 'Whatever brings money to the town does good eventually to all inhabitants engaged in trade', the *Stirling Journal* insisted in 1864 when appealing for donations to set up a Stirling regatta. 'It is a duty to give ample facilities for bowling, cricket, curling, tennis, golf, etc. so as to induce visitors to come and bring prosperity', Provost Philp of Bridge of Allan noted in 1897. For the promoters of bowling greens like that at the Mine House, Bridge of Allan, of Highland Games gatherings like Strathallan and of golf courses like those at Aberfoyle, Alva, Balfron, Bridge of Allan, Callander, Drymen, Milngavie and Tillicoultry, the principal objective was to attract residents and visitors in order to advance the collective prosperity of the communities in which they lived (Tranter, 1989a: 245, 247).

How far sport succeeded in fulfilling the various intentions of its participants and patrons remains one of the most under-researched topics in its history. How much the growing participation in sport contributed to improvements in the quality of life and to changes in the extent to which individuals identified with group and place, and how much the growing participation in sport contributed to these trends, are questions that it may never be possible to answer effectively. In the course of the Victorian and Edwardian periods concern for individual and community status certainly increased and, as it was intended to do, a greater association with sport no doubt made some contribution to this. To date, however, it is impossible to determine how significant this contribution was relative to the many other ways in which individuals and communities sought to display and enhance their standing.

To judge from the evidence of increasing average height and falling rates of mortality, standards of health improved markedly during the late nineteenth and early twentieth centuries, particularly in urban areas. But here, too, the contribution made by a wider participation in sport is difficult to assess. Currently, all that can be said is that it was probably far smaller than those who advocated sport as a panacea for poor physical health had hoped. Much of the rise in health standards that had occurred by 1914 was the result of influences affecting infants and young children, who did not participate in sport. And even for older children and adults the contribution of sport to health was probably dwarfed by the impact of improvements in public health conditions and nutrition, and further diminished by the fact that an active participation in sport was always confined to a minority.

By the beginning of the twentieth century, indeed, many contemporary commentators were questioning the assumption that sport was necessarily conducive to higher standards of physical, mental and moral well-being. Fuelled by defeats in the Boer War and increasing anxiety over the rise of foreign industrial and imperialist competition, the conviction grew that what appeared to be a national obsession with sport was in danger of becoming counter-productive. Arthur Shadwell was not alone in believing that 'we are a nation at play. Work is a nuisance, an evil necessity to be shirked and hurried over as quickly and easily as possible in order that we may get away to the real business of life – the golf course, the bridge table, the cricket and football field or some other of the thousand amusements which occupy our minds'. The poor physical state of recruits to the armed services and the forced closure of works and shops caused by widespread absenteeism among workers at times of major sporting events no doubt helped confirm the growing belief that, in practice, sport was failing to produce a population sufficiently fit in body and mind to meet the needs of the military for soldiers and of industry for labourers (Mason, 1982: 262–3; Huggins, 1987: 112; Birley, 1995: 230). Particular attention was devoted to the harm sport was assumed to be wreaking among the nation's military and economic leadership. An overindulgence in sport, it was increasingly claimed, had distracted businessmen from their work, undermined the will of the leisured classes to fight and led to the neglect of genuine physical exercise and a training in the specific skills needed on the modern battle-field. Moreover, through its emphasis on team games and on par-ticipation rather than playing to win, it encouraged conformity and cooperation instead of the qualities of individualism and indepen-dent initiative that were so crucial for successful military and busi-ness leadership (Lowerson, 1993: 278–88).

Historians nowadays would generally consider these claims to be unfounded or, at least, exaggerated. Compared with those of France and Germany, the quality of Britain's ordinary soldiers was relatively low. But this was more a reflection of the British army's reliance on volunteers not conscripts than of lower standards of health among its military recruits. Judging from data on average heights, these standards were actually higher in the Edwardian period than ever before and compared favourably with those of other European countries. The belief that sport, played according to the tenets of the public-school games' ideology, was an adequate preparation for military leadership may go some way towards explaining why officers in the British army lacked the professional-ism and skills of their German counterparts.

But such comparative failings probably owed more to a combi-nation of the peculiarities of the British class system, a general sus-picion of specialism in all walks of life and a belief that what had worked in the past would continue to work in the future. An earlier consensus in favour of an overall decline in the quality of British business entrepreneurship during late Victorian and Edwardian times is either rejected outright or, at best, regarded as not proven by more recent economic historians. And even if standards of busi-ness leadership did decline it is unlikely that either an excessive indulgence in sport or the kind of values learned from sport would figure among its principal explanations. First, there is no firm empirical evidence to support the view that entrepreneurs devoted too much time to sport and too little to business. Secondly, only a small minority of the entrepreneurs in manufacturing industry, against whom accusations of incompetence are most often directed, attended the elite public schools and ancient universities where the emphasis on sport and the 'amateur' ideal was strongest. In any case, those that did, though unlikely to receive an education which positively encouraged them to take up a career in manufac-turing, found themselves in an environment far from hostile to the pursuit of industrial success and capable of instilling many of the qualities – self-confidence, determination and resilience – essential to its achievement. Thirdly, by the 1890s and 1900s the availability of scientific and technical subjects in the curricula of universities, colleges and schools was increasing so rapidly that the supply of students with the type of academic qualifications most directly relevant to the needs of industry far exceeded demand. In elite Scottish schools, in particular, headmasters like John Guthrie Kerr of Allan Glen's made every effort to ensure that sport was not pursued to the detriment of a training in applied science and technology (Mangan, 1988: 92–3). Finally, to suggest that sport was harmful to standards of entrepreneurship is to ignore the fact that in the commercial and financial sectors of the economy, where many of those most influenced by the public-school games' cult were employed, the quality of business leadership was undeniably high. How far this reflected the influence of the games' cult and how far the influence of other forces is an issue that remains to be more carefully investigated.

Further research is also needed to determine the extent to which expectations of making money from working or investing in sport and its ancillary industries were matched in reality. It is, however, already clear that for only a fraction of paid employees and investors were the rewards from sport exceptionally high. At the peak of his career Fred Archer, the champion jockey, earned between £8,000 and £13,000 a year. By the last two decades of the nineteenth century at least ten other jockeys were earning over £5,000 a season. Even a moderately successful jockey could make £1,000 or more in a good year. Over the period 1870–1910 W. G. Grace is thought to have earned £120,000 directly and indirectly from cricket (Vamplew, 1976: 145–8; 1988b: 201, 217).

Very few sportsmen made fortunes of this magnitude. None the less, the earnings of leading performers were often substantial. Professional anglers like Walter Darwin and Joseph Bradshaw are reputed to have made considerable amounts of money from side-stake matches and exhibitions (Lowerson, 1988: 122). In the five years preceding December 1844 the Scottish quoiter, David Weir, is reported to have earned over £900 for himself and his backers. Between 1861 and 1868 Robert Walkinshaw made six successful defences of his British quoiting championship, for total stakes of

£800 (Tranter, 1990a: 56–7). The best professional bowlers could earn up to £800 a year and some golf professionals around £300 (Lowerson, 1993: 175, 197). On average, the basic annual earnings of a county cricket professional rose from £100 in 1870 to £275 in 1900, by which time they were over twice as high as those of most skilled workers and roughly three times higher than those of an unskilled worker. On top of this, the more successful professionals could expect extra income from bonuses for outstanding performances and from appearances in representative matches, overseas tours and coaching contracts and the award of a benefit for long and distinguished service. Fees for representative games ranged from £6 to £10 throughout the second half of the nineteenth century to £20 after 1899. Overseas coaching contracts typically paid £4 or £5 a week plus a benefit match. In the 1860s members of overseas touring teams earned between £90 and £475: tourists to Australia in 1882 around £200 net. For first-class cricketers lucky enough to be awarded a benefit by their counties the average return rose from £200 in 1870 to £600 by 1900, though the range varied greatly, from as low as £80 for Figg in 1872 and Humphrey in 1891 to £2,282 for Brown in 1901 and a record £3,073 for Hirst in 1904. At this level of earning it is little wonder that competition for a county contract was so intense (Mandle, 1973: 6–7, 9–11; Vamplew, 1988b: 218–22; Sandiford, 1994: 85, 89, 101).

The earnings of leading soccer players were equally substantial and, as in the case of 'star' cricketers, well above those of unskilled workers and even of the skilled workers from whose ranks most of them were drawn. Down to the early 1890s top soccer players earned from £1 10s to £2 a week in season. In 1893 this was raised to £3 or £4 and £2 a week out of season. By the end of the century 'stars' were earning £6 or £7 and other leading players £4 a week during the playing months. In 1903 the English FA introduced a maximum weekly wage of £4, raised to £5 for senior players six years later. In Scotland, where there was no maximum wage legislation, a handful of top 'stars' were also earning £4 or £5 a week by the Edwardian period. For players at the pinnacle of the profession, moreover, earnings were considerably increased by signing-on fees, sometimes in excess of the legally permissible maximum of £10, job sinecures, low-rent accommodation, appearances in international matches, payments for which rose from £1 in 1887 to £4 by 1908, and benefits, which varied from £100 in the Southern League to £150-200 and occasionally up to £500 in the Football League (Vamplew, 1988b: 222, 224; Mason, 1989b: 160; Holt, 1989: 288, 293–4). Admittedly, few even of soccer's most successful players received such perks or earned the maximum wage. In 1905, for instance, the majority of first-team players at West Ham United were paid an average of just £2 10s a week over the whole year. Yet even this exceeded the earnings of skilled workers like joiners and plumbers (£2 7s), tramdrivers (£2 3s) and building tradesmen (£2 8s), and far exceeded the 5s 6d to £1 2s 6d earned each week by casual dockworkers (Korr, 1978: 228–9).

For the vast bulk of sport's paid employees, however, the reality was very different. Most golf professionals had little or no job security and in the 1890s were earning between just ten shillings and £1 a week. Even with additional income from tuition fees and the sale of balls and clubs the earnings of the typical golf professional were lower than those of schoolteachers and skilled workers. At best, golf caddies earned six shillings a week, roughly the same as a casual agricultural worker: gamekeepers about £1 a week, higher than most unskilled workers but low by the standards of the skilled; apprentice jockeys between nine and thirteen guineas a year, stable lads between forty and fifty guineas. Very few professionals were able to make a decent living out of soccer. Benefit matches were at the discretion of the club they played for and, in practice, were awarded to only a small number of 'star' players. Of 6,800 soccer professionals in England in 1910 only 573 earned the maximum wage. Even at clubs as wealthy as Glasgow Rangers most first-team players were paid just £2 a week and reserve-team players £1. For part-time players at clubs like Cowdenbeath weekly wages never exceeded fifteen shillings, with nothing paid in the close season. Broken-time payments in rugby league were initially fixed at a maximum of six shillings a game. By 1900 leading players were earning between thirty shillings and £4 a week. But no payment was allowed out of season and the majority of rugby league professionals earned considerably less (Vamplew, 1988b: 210–11, 217, 224; Holt, 1989: 293; Lowerson, 1989a: 196; 1993: 192, 195, 198).

The earnings of most county cricket professionals fell well short of those of cricket's top performers. Seven of the 24 professionals employed by Lancashire in 1899 earned less than £3 a week in season, eleven received nothing out of season and all were expected to pay their own travel and accommodation costs. Benefits were awarded only to the handful of players who served their counties for exceptionally long periods – in the case of Yorkshire, for example, for an average of thirteen years. Below the level of the journeyman county professional earnings were lower still. In the 1890s the typical club professional earned around £80 a year, supplemented by occasional modest bonuses and collections and rarely more than £20 from a benefit match. Ground staff professionals hired by clubs like Surrey and the MCC to bowl at members in the nets were usually paid between thirty and fifty shillings a week, but only during the season. For the ordinary professional cricketer, as for the majority of professionals in other sports, earnings were moderate (Mandle, 1973: 1, 6–7, 12, 15; Vamplew, 1988b: 222, 226; Holt, 1989: 288–9; Sandiford, 1994: 87–90).

Worse still, very few of those who aspired to become professional sportsmen managed to achieve their ambition. And, for the minority who did, careers were invariably brief. No more than 10 per cent of all caddies became golf professionals (Lowerson, 1993: 198). Of the fifty colts who applied to the Yorkshire County Cricket Club in 1904 only seven were taken on as full-time professionals and only three survived more than one season. Of 502 professionals registered with English first-division soccer clubs in 1891–2 43 per cent did not play a single first-team match. Just 40 per cent of the 187 apprentice jockeys registered in 1900 became licensed jockeys and just 47 per cent of all rugby league professionals, 45 per cent of all first-class cricket professionals and 12 per cent of all professional jockeys had careers lasting longer than three years. Nearly half of all English first-division soccer players were discarded after one season and over three-quarters after two seasons (Vamplew, 1988b: 207, 228, 233).

For the overwhelming majority of men who aspired to the status of professional sportsman the reality of opportunity and reward was a far cry from the achievements of the few. While the growth of the sports' industry undoubtedly extended the range of occupations open to working-class males, in terms of the wages they paid these occupations were at best only marginally more rewarding than others they might have followed. For most of sport's paid employees work was arduous, playing careers brief and, compared with many working-class occupations, relatively insecure. At a time when the status accorded to a professional sportsman differed little from that of a servant or labourer and supply far exceeded demand it could not have been otherwise (Mandle, 1973: 13; Vamplew, 1988b: 211, 227; Mason, 1989b: 160; Holt, 1989: 288; Lowerson, 1993: 191; Sandiford, 1994: 80, 83, 85). Furthermore, only a small proportion of even the most highly acclaimed and better-paid professionals used their money and fame to establish themselves as successful businessmen once they had retired from sport. For every case like that of the angler Walter Darwin, who became a prosperous fishing-tackle dealer, there are numerous cases of others who, lacking the savings and prestige of the most illustrious performers and burdened by the working-class preference for living for the present rather than the future, either returned to the occupation they had originally followed or, in far too many instances, ended their days in poverty. In reality, few of those who had been paid to play it were able to utilise sport as a vehicle for subsequent material and social advancement (Mandle, 1973: 10, 14; Vamplew, 1976: 171–2; 1988b: 233, 235, 237; Lowerson, 1989b: 28; 1993, 197–8; Sandiford, 1994: 27, 104–6).

Such fragmentary data as we have on the returns made by those who invested rather than actively participated in sport indicate that here too only a minority profited substantially from their investment. In the sport of horseracing this minority included men like Lord Boyne at Stockton and A. H. T. Newcomen and Lord Zetland at Redcar, owners of the land on which courses were built, hoteliers such as J. Wilstrop and the Hickeley family, who hosted race dinners, some of the breeders of brood mares and, to judge from the average dividend of 7.5 per cent paid out in 1913 (well above the 3.4 per cent paid on consols), the bulk of shareholders in racecourse companies. Similarly healthy dividends were paid to shareholders in ice-rink companies and in some of the other sports companies which gave priority to profit rather than utility maximisation. The majority of those who invested in sport, however, did less well. In a period when the amount of prize money per horse was falling and the cost of training fees, jockeys' retainers and bloodstock rising, few breeders of stallions and very few racehorse owners made other than losses (Vamplew, 1976: 191–2; 1988b, 100, 103, 105, 107, 109; 1989, 217, 227–8, 230; Huggins, 1987: 112, 115).

The financial returns to directors and shareholders in soccer clubs were far outweighed by the risks (Arnold, 1989: 325). In the season 1908–9 only six of England's sixty-two leading soccer clubs paid shareholders a dividend. In Scotland the only soccer clubs to pay a dividend before 1914 were Rangers and Celtic. Payments to directors were prohibited by the English FA and in Scotland, where they were legal, were offered only once before 1914 – at Celtic in 1913 when each senior director received £50 (Holt, 1989: 283; Mason, 1989b: 164). How far the absence of dividends was compensated by indirect earnings from contracts for building and maintenance work and the provision of equipment and refreshments is unclear. Examples like those of Archibald Leitch of Glasgow Rangers, who designed the new Ibrox stadium, and the Penman brothers, who supplied Glasgow Celtic with its playing kit, indicate that there were certainly some shareholders who profited indirectly. But how common such examples were we do not yet know. At least one historian has argued that they were exceptional and that, generally, shareholders neither made, nor expected to make, an indirect profit from their involvement (Holt, 1989: 283). Another has suggested that such direct and indirect returns as were made by investors in soccer clubs may in any case have been more than outweighed by the willingness of some of the largest shareholders to use their non-soccer income to support the club they invested in (Tischler, 1981: 76).

The infrequency with which investors received dividends by no means always reflected the low profitability of the sporting organisations in which they invested. On the contrary, some organisations generated substantial levels of profit. The West Ham United Football Club, for example, reported a profit in every season from 1905 to 1914, though not until 1911 did assets exceed liabilities (Korr, 1978: 227). In 1904–5 the Aston Villa FC made net profits of over £3,376. During the years immediately prior to the outbreak of the First World War annual net profits averaged £3,282 at Tottenham Hotspur, £2,872 at Liverpool, £2,551 at Burnley, £1,550 at Blackburn Rovers and £1,241 at Glasgow Celtic. In the season 1913–14 the average level of profit among eight English first-division soccer clubs was as high as £5,823 (Vamplew, 1988b: 64; Murray, 1994: 27). For cricket clubs like the MCC, Lancashire, Nottinghamshire, Surrey, Yorkshire and, to a lesser extent,

Kent income exceeded expenditure throughout the period between the 1890s and 1914. In 1899 the Lancashire County Cricket Club declared net profits of almost £2,000: in 1894, despite an expenditure of £1,500, the Liverpool club a profit of £282. And many clubs – Halifax, Wimbledon and the Church Hill club of Bradford among them – were sufficiently prosperous to employ professional players (Sandiford and Vamplew, 1986: 312; Vamplew, 1988b: 93–4; Sandiford, 1994: 57–8, 69). By 1906 the Oldham Rugby League Club had £1,500 invested in loan funds, the Hull Rugby League Club owed less than £2,500 on ground improvements costing £12,000 and the Bradford Rugby League Club a mortgage of just £7,000 on facilities valued at £25,000 (Vamplew, 1988b: 65). In the case of bowling, curling and golf clubs, too, evidence for the Stirling region of Scotland suggests that ordinary annual income invariably exceeded ordinary annual expenditure and that, on the whole, the capital required for extraordinary expenditures, on new clubhouses and the like, was easily raised and speedily repaid (Tranter, 1990c: 379–82). With only occasional exceptions, profits also appear to have been the norm among racecourse companies (Vamplew, 1976: 38–48; 1988b: 57).

As a general rule though, even in sports which put profit maximisation ahead of utility maximisation, the majority of sporting institutions either failed to make a profit or generated profits that were too low or too irregular to pay investors a dividend. In 1911–12 the average level of profit among twenty Northern Rugby Union clubs was as low as £174 (Vamplew, 1988b: 99). Between 1890 and 1899, despite the claim of its committee that 'first and foremost we are businessmen', the net annual balance of the Strathallan Highland Games averaged only £238. Over the period 1872–85 the average annual excess of income over expenditure achieved by the Alloa Games was a mere £51 and on the eve of the Alloa Games of 1890, 1899 and 1900 the committee reported favourable balances of just £40, £59 and £57 respectively. At these and other Highland Games gatherings profits were rarely better than moderate.

In the two most popular and commercialised spectator sports, cricket and soccer, profits of any kind were unusual. Until the 1890s, it is true, most soccer clubs had little difficulty balancing their books. With the coming of professionalism, the growing intensity of competition between clubs for spectators and the escalating costs of providing facilities to cope with ever-larger crowds the situation altered dramatically. Except for a few clubs operating at the very highest level, by the close of the Victorian era debt was the norm and survival usually precarious (Vamplew, 1988b: 64; Metcalfe, 1988: 275–9; Arnold, 1989: 327–9, 331; Tranter, 1990c: 382–4). In the case of cricket, where competition from other sports was fiercer and little effort was made to attract spectators, even at the highest levels of the game the majority of clubs found it impossible to balance income and expenditure and survived thanks only to the generosity of members and patrons (Sandiford and Vamplew, 1986: 312–13; Vamplew, 1988b: 59; J. Williams, 1989: 121, 123; Tranter, 1990c: 382; Sandiford, 1994: 55, 58, 65, 68, 115, 121–2).

With some justification, Vamplew has concluded that the emergence of a mass sports industry was one of the 'economic success stories' of late Victorian and Edwardian Britain, yet another example of an industry which fails to conform to the charge that, generally, the country's industrial entrepreneurs were incapable of branching out into new technologies and activities (Vamplew, 1982: 549–50). Partly because of deficiencies in the surviving statistical data and partly because of the difficulty in determining the degree to which investment in sport diverted resources from activities that may have yielded larger and more lasting benefits to the economy, to go beyond this and attempt to assess the precise extent of the industry's impact on the economy as a whole is no easy task. At present, all that can be concluded with any safety is that an industry which may have accounted for no more than 3 per cent of total gross national product could hardly have had other than a modest effect on the overall performance of the economy. At best it acted only as a partial counterbalance to the retardation which is supposed to have occurred elsewhere in the manufacturing sector (Lowerson, 1993: 225–6, 248): at worst it merely aggravated such reluctance as there was to invest adequately in other new but more productive technologies and industries.

In the context of regional economies the impact of the sports industry was inevitably larger. From the examples of horserace meetings on Tees-side, Highland Games gatherings in Scotland, municipal golf courses in places like Bournemouth, the manufacture

of cycles and golf equipment in Coventry and the impact of commercial sport in cities like Glasgow, historians have frequently
argued that the rise of the sports industry had significant, material
benefits for the communities in which it was most concentrated
(Huggins, 1987: 111; Lowerson, 1993: 134, 226). To date, however,
little work has been done to measure the exact extent of these benefits. Willie Orr's study of the economic impact of deer forests in the
Scottish Highlands is an all-too-rare exception. In the five west
Highland counties where it was chiefly centred, expenditures on
deerstalking went some way towards replacing the employment,
rental income and local purchasing power lost as a result of the
decline in commercial sheep farming brought about by increasing
imports of sheep and sheep products from Australia and New
Zealand. At the height of their popularity deer forests accounted for
between a quarter and a third of the total capital value of the regions
in which they were located. Despite this, their benefits to the local
economy should not be overstated. For one thing, the amount of
employment they created probably fell well short of that previously
generated by sheep farming. For another, only part of the income
earned by Highland landlords from the influx of sportsmen was
spent locally. Fundamentally, the western Highlands remained an
under-developed region, the main function of which was to provide
a reserve army of cheap labour for other regions of Britain and
economies overseas. None the less, Orr concludes, the economy of
the western Highlands would certainly have been considerably
poorer in the absence of the deerstalking industry (Orr, 1982:
90–118, 147–8). Whether or not other sports industries elsewhere
had comparable effects has still to be investigated.

In an industry more subject than most to the vagaries of consumer choice and fierce inter-firm rivalry it is only to be expected
that many of the companies drawn into the provision of goods and
services for sport's players and their supporters were short-lived.
Hampered by the persistence of outdated handicraft techniques,
the limited size of the domestic market, the additional costs
imposed by the gun licence tax and, above all, by competition from
larger and more efficient firms both at home and overseas, many of
the smaller companies producing guns for the cheaper end of the
market soon disappeared. In London the number of gun-manufac-
turing firms fell from sixty-three in 1880 to twenty in 1906:

Birmingham's gun output fell by a half; and the profits made by Eley's, manufacturers of cartridges, fell from 25 per cent in the 1880s to 5 per cent in 1904.

Most of the small family firms which had met the initial demand for cycles were forced out of business in the late 1880s and 1890s by an inability to adopt the new technologies and production methods required by pneumatically tyred cycles. Many others disappeared following the collapse of the cycle boom of 1895–7 and most of the rest survived on the slenderest of profit margins.

With the adoption of the Haskell ball by Edwardian golfers, the supply of golf balls came to be dominated by large companies like Dunlop and the North British Rubastic Company whose resources were sufficient to permit the introduction of the large-scale, machine-based production methods its rubber-strip core demanded. Less well-capitalised or less enterprising firms like the Anglo-French Golf Ball Manufacturing Company of Bristol were unable to compete and the failure rate among the numerous small companies trying to find a niche in the market was high. Whether because of poor marketing, undercapitalisation or, more commonly, a lack of advertising revenue, many of the specialist newspapers and periodicals launched to cash in on the demand for sporting news, like the *All England Cricket and Football Journal and Athletic Review* (1878–9), were also short-lived. Between 1870 and 1914 at least twenty-nine cycling publications failed in the London area alone. Outside London the chances of establishing a successful sports publication were even more limited (Lowerson, 1989a: 195; 1993, 232–3, 235–6, 238–9, 253–4).

Set against the failures, of course, are the many firms that clearly managed to profit from the sports boom: Duke's of Penshurst, which evolved from the small workshop production of hand-sewn cricket balls in the 1760s to a factory-sized organisation in 1880; Wisden's, which opened its first cricket ball factory at Tonbridge in 1890; John Jaques and Son of London, which moved into the production of ping-pong equipment and by 1912 was valued at £35,000; Hardy's of Alnwick, manufacturers of fishing tackle, which had a capital value of nearly £70,000 by 1907; gunmaking firms like Elderkin's of Spalding, Purdey's of London and Westley Richards of Birmingham; Dunlop's and the North British Rubastic Company, manufacturers of golf balls; and Fred Hopper and Company of Barton-on-Humber, Lincolnshire, cycle manufacturer. In 1901 Slazenger's, which specialised in the production of lawn tennis equipment, reported a profit of £26,867. By 1910 this had risen to £38,836 and by 1913, following its conversion into a public company, to £49,226 (Lowerson, 1993: 227–9, 231–2, 235, 237–8).

For companies like William Shillcock, football outfitters, W. Herbert Fowler and Thomas C. Simpson, golf course developers, Fred Braby, manufacturers of roofing, railings and wirenetting and the supplier of materials for the new Ibrox stadium, and Duncan's, which built it, and for men like the Glasgow engineer, William McLean, who began producing 'St Vincent' cycles in 1893 and within four years was employing forty men, sport was obviously a lucrative business (Vamplew, 1988b: 55; Lowerson, 1993: 242). In contrast to the many sports publications that failed were the many others that succeeded – among them, *The Field, Horse and Hound, Baily's Magazine of Sports and Pastimes, C. B. Fry's Magazine of Sports and Outdoor Life, The Fishing Gazette, Cycling* and *Golf Illustrated*. Railway and tram companies profited from the carriage of spectators to sporting events, the Post Office from the increased use of the telegraph service, tobacconists and newsagents from acting as distributors of tickets and programmes, newspapers from the insatiable demand for sports news and printing firms from the demands made on them to satisfy it (Vamplew, 1988b: 55–6; Lowerson, 1993: 251–3).

That the Victorian and Edwardian sporting 'revolution' was a profitable experience for many of the companies which supplied the equipment and services it required is indisputable. It is impossible to say whether the number of companies which responded successfully to the new opportunities exceeded the unsuccessful. Nor do we yet know enough about the levels of profitability achieved or how these compared with those in other areas of commercial and industrial activity. On both matters further research is urgently required in order to provide a more satisfactory understanding than we have at present of the financial cost–benefit of sport for the individuals, organisations and communities who participated and invested in it and for the economy as a whole. How far the participation in sport succeeded in fulfilling the objectives of those people and organisations whose principal motives for involvement were other than financial gain may well prove an even more difficult matter to resolve.

6

No place for women?

All historians are agreed that the Victorian and Edwardian 'revolution' in sport was predominantly a male phenomenon in which females, and working-class females especially, had relatively little part. Fragmentary though it is, there is sufficient evidence to suggest that in earlier ages working-class women were more frequent participants in sport. At various times between the seventeenth and early nineteenth centuries they were regularly recorded among the crowds at horseraces, cricket matches, rowing and pedestrian events and at animal blood sports like bull-baiting and combat sports like prize-fighting, wrestling, sword-fighting and cudgelling. In the sports of football, rowing, cricket and, occasionally, prize-fighting some even participated actively (Guttmann, 1985: 105–7, 116–17; 1991, 71–9; Wigglesworth, 1986: 148; Huggins, 1987: 101; Brailsford, 1991: 74, 78–9, 131, 133). Because of the scattered and imprecise nature of the evidence, the extent of this participation cannot be quantified exactly. But the general assumption is that it was more extensive than it was to be in Victorian and Edwardian times. Apart from women's continued involvement in street games during childhood, a moderate and variable level of attendance at regattas and Highland Games gatherings and a possible increase in their numbers at horse race meetings, by the beginning of the Victorian period working-class females had largely disappeared from the crowds at sporting events, particularly from those of a more violent kind like prize-fighting. By the third quarter of the nineteenth century there were no female pugilists and the number of working-class women actively participating in sports such as cricket, football, footracing and other forms of pedestrianism was negligible (Guttmann, 1985: 111; Brailsford, 1991, 133–6; Murray, 1994: 49).

In the course of the later decades of the century there are signs that the involvement of lower-class females in sport slowly began to increase. Stimulated by growing concerns for labour productivity and national efficiency, racial regeneration and moral welfare, from the late 1870s onwards gymnastic exercises for girls were introduced into the curricula of elementary schools. At the same time organisations like the National Association of Working Girls' Clubs, the Girls' Guilds, the YWCA and the Girl Guides, together with one or two of the more enlightened employers like Cadbury and Rowntree, began to provide sports like hockey, swimming and various forms of athletics for their female members and employees to enjoy (Holt, 1989: 118; McCrone, 1991: 159, 161, 165, 172, 174, 178–9; Hargreaves, 1994: 110–11). By the start of the Edwardian era, working-class women were setting up their own hockey clubs, regularly watching league cricket in the north and midlands and, though less extensively in Scotland than England, were once again present in reasonable numbers among the spectators at soccer matches (Hay, 1982: 234; McCrone, 1991: 170–1; Williams and Woodhouse, 1991: 89).

Overall, however, the impact of these developments was minimal. While it is wrong to imply, as some historians have, that working-class females were entirely excluded from an active participation in the new world of organised sport (Clarke and Crichter, 1985: 70; Williams and Woodhouse, 1991: 89; Warren, 1993: 59, 62), there is no doubt that their participation was restricted to no more than a tiny minority (McCrone, 1991: 181; Hargreaves, 1994: 68, 107–8). In contrast to their middle-class counterparts, working-class women rarely fished, much less frequently cycled and never took part in organised games of cricket and football (Rubinstein, 1977: 59; Lowerson, 1988: 118; Sandiford, 1994: 48; Murray, 1994: 49). Inhibited by low incomes, a persisting subservience to their fathers and husbands and the absence of a tradition of sport at school, and drained of energy and time for leisure by the rigours of domestic life and employment, few working-class women were in a position to take advantage of the sporting 'revolution'. Possibly, with more support from their middle-class sisters, things might have been different. But, as the case of hockey graphically illustrates, middle-class women were reluctant to share their leisure activities with their social inferiors and, on balance, preferred to oppose rather than encourage the latter's efforts to become involved (Guttmann, 1991: 106; McCrone, 1991: 159–60, 165, 169–72, 179–80). To the extent that there was an increase in the participation of females in sport during the later Victorian and Edwardian eras the increase was limited almost entirely to the middle-class (Holt, 1989: 118, 130; Brailsford, 1991: 137).

Implicitly if not explicitly, earlier scholars of women's cultural and social experiences in nineteenth-century Britain argued that, with only occasional exceptions, upper- and middle-class females, too, indulged in little physical exercise and certainly had no place in the public world of sport and physical recreation (Branca, 1978: 194; Duffin, 1978: 39). More recent work, while acknowledging that the extent of their involvement was modest and perhaps more restricted through much of the nineteenth century than in previous centuries (McCrone, 1987: 99, 103; Brailsford, 1991: 133, 136), has somewhat modified this view. By the last decade or so of the Victorian period, it is now agreed, upper- and middle-class females were more extensively involved in sporting activities outside the confines of the home and garden than it was once customary for historians to suppose (Parratt, 1989: 141–2; Tranter, 1989b: 33).

Beginning around the middle of the nineteenth century the extent of elite female participation in the public world of organised physical recreation steadily increased. The trend originated and proceeded furthest among girls at public schools, colleges and universities. Initially, such physical exercise as was permitted in the new girls' public schools was restricted to gentle forms of callisthenic activity like crocodile walks and dancing. From the 1870s and 1880s these rapidly gave way first to more robust forms of gymnastic exercise, based on the Swedish model, and then to an ever-widening array of individual and team sports, many of them calling for considerable expenditures of physical energy and, through sophisticated structures of inter-form, inter-house and inter-school competition, practised in a highly competitive manner. Similar developments occurred in the physical education and teacher training colleges, the London polytechnics and the universities.

By the end of the century elite female school and college students had the opportunity to participate in a range of sports and physical recreations unimaginable only a quarter of a century earlier – archery, athletics, basketball and netball, battledore and shuttlecock and its modern variant badminton, cricket, cycling, fencing, fives, golf, hockey, lacrosse, lawn tennis, ninepins, ping-pong, quoits, rounders, roller-skating, swimming and ice-skating. By 1914 probably a majority of the female offspring of upper- and middle-class parents had responded to the opportunity and participated at least occasionally in some form of reasonably energetic physical recreation while at school or college. For the daughters of the social elites the provision of facilities for sport in educational establishments had become common and sport was now accepted as a permissible, if not an essential, part of their training for life (Atkinson, 1978: 92–3, 113; McCrone, 1987: 103, 105; 1988: 21–126; 1990, 205; Holt, 1989: 118–21; Guttmann, 1991: 106–17; Warren, 1993: 55–6; Hargreaves, 1994: 56–7, 63, 68, 103–5).

Outside the institutions of education progress was slower and less pervasive. Yet here, too, the late nineteenth and early twentieth centuries saw significant changes. For much of the first three-quarters of the nineteenth century the only publicly pursued sports to attract substantial numbers of elite, adult female players were croquet, which first became popular in the 1850s and 1860s, and archery, a sport long practised by aristocratic women but not widely adopted by middle-class women until the 1860s. Both sports allowed men and women to play together and included a modest element of competitiveness in their essentially social and recreational nature. But neither required more than a moderate amount of physical exertion. For all but a handful of upper- and middle-class women the public world of organised sport, particularly that of a vigorous, predominantly competitive and team-based kind, remained firmly closed (McCrone, 1988: 288; Tranter, 1989b: 36; Lowerson, 1993: 208–9; Hargreaves, 1994: 88–9, 98–9).

In the period between the 1870s/1880s and 1914 the situation changed in two important respects. First, the number of elite females actively participating in sport during adulthood markedly increased. Secondly, the nature of their participation began to alter, away from a preference for largely casual, recreational and gentle forms of sport towards a preference for more institutionalised forms of involvement, based around formally constituted club structures and governing bodies, and for sports which

provided greater opportunities for competitiveness and more rigorous physical exertion.

In the current state of knowledge it is impossible to be precise
about the magnitude of these changes. But there is no doubt that
they occurred. One authority has claimed that by the beginning of
the Edwardian era upper- and middle-class women were already
actively participating in nearly thirty different sports (Parratt,
1989, 144). True, in many of these – archery, athletics, bowls,
hunting, netball, punting, riding, rifle-shooting, rounders and
roller-skating among them – levels of participation, though generally higher than ever before, remained low and progress towards
formalised, competitive structures painfully slow. In the sports of
archery and punting national championships for ladies were first
introduced in the 1880s. The first competitive ice-skating event for
women, however, did not occur until 1906 (Hargreaves, 1994: 99).
Female swimmers were first admitted to national swimming championships in Scotland in 1892 and in England in 1901, but in both
cases only to a narrow range of events and, along with female rowers and athletes, they were excluded from participation in the London Olympics of 1908 (Holt, 1989: 130; Hargreaves, 1994: 102;
Birley, 1995: 220–1). Women do not appear to have competed in
the grand bonspiels organised by the Royal Caledonian Curling
Club until that of 1898–9, and even then only two took part. Of
the five hundred or so curling clubs in Scotland in 1899 only two
were composed entirely of females and only a further twenty-two
included women among their members (Tranter, 1989b: 36). By
1906 female bowlers were sufficiently numerous in southern England for the London County Council to set aside one rink in each
of its seventy-six public parks for their exclusive use. In northern
England, by contrast, they were far less common. Few bowling
clubs had women's sections, mixed-sex bowling was a rarity and
the first all-female bowling club, at Kington Canonbury in Surrey,
was not opened until 1910 (Birley, 1995: 206).

Rounders and netball were among many women's sports where
levels of participation were too low to permit the establishment of
a national governing body before the 1920s (Hargreaves, 1994:
102). The eleven women's clubs affiliated to the National Rifle
Association in 1913 had a total of just 292 members (Lowerson,
1993: 219). In spite of its popularity in the schools and colleges,

lacrosse was another sport which females rarely continued into adulthood. The first women's lacrosse club, the London-based Southern Ladies, was not formed until 1905. Not until 1912, when the sport's governing body was established, was a second club formed, in Edinburgh, and not until 1913 was the first international match (England versus Scotland) played (McCrone, 1988: 138–41). Despite the efforts of Nettie Honeyball and the British Ladies' Football Club to promote professional female soccer in the mid-1890s and of Lady Florence Dixey, the organiser of women's exhibition soccer matches in Scotland in the early 1900s (Williams and Woodhouse: 1991, 90), soccer, too, failed to attract significant numbers of active female participants. Cricket was only marginally more successful. The formation of the first female cricket club, the White Heather Club at Nun Appleton, Yorkshire, in 1887, was not followed by a sustained growth in the sport's popularity among women. In subsequent years a number of clubs came and went without ever securing cricket as a major female participant sport. The establishment of two teams of female professionals in 1890 ended after just one season when its (male) promoters absconded with the funds. The experiment was never repeated. As late as the Edwardian period there was just one female cricket club for every fifty female hockey clubs. Not until 1926 was women's cricket sufficiently developed to permit the formation of a national governing body. Despite their considerable presence among the crowds at first-class cricket matches and in the membership of English county cricket clubs, few upper- and middle-class women actually played the game (McCrone, 1988: 145, 153; Hargreaves, 1994: 102; Sandiford, 1994: 44, 47).

It is to the sports of golf, hockey, lawn tennis and, to a lesser extent, badminton, cycling and, particularly after 1906, ice-skating that we must turn for clearest confirmation of the growing involvement of elite women in competitive, institutionalised sport. Badminton emerged from the old game of battledore and shuttlecock in the 1870s and rapidly established itself as a popular female sport. Women first participated in publicly organised badminton competitions in 1900 and by 1914 were extensively represented in the 250 or so clubs affiliated to the Badminton Association (Holt, 1989: 125; Hargreaves, 1994: 99). From its inception in 1880, the Cyclists' Touring Club, in common with most other cycling clubs, encouraged females to join. But it was only from the 1890s, as a result of the cheaper and more practical cycles made possible by the technological innovations of the previous decade, that the popularity of cycling among middle-class women dramatically increased. Thereafter, although rarely participating in competitive events, women remained numerous in the membership of cycling clubs, either in separate sections of predominantly male clubs or, less frequently, in clubs restricted to their own sex (McCrone, 1988: 182–3; Hargreaves, 1994: 94).

The sports of lawn tennis, golf and hockey also attracted substantial and increasing numbers of active adult female participants. Between 1900 and 1914 the number of clubs affiliated to the Lawn Tennis Association rose from 300 to around 11,000 (Holt, 1989: 126). Since in most lawn tennis clubs the number of females equalled or exceeded the number of males, this reflects a healthy growth in women's participation in the sport. The first all-female golf club, founded at St Andrews in 1867, already had 500 members by the 1880s. In England institutional golf for women began in 1868 with the establishment of the Westward Ho and North Devon Ladies' Golf Club. Most of the clubs which opened in subsequent years were basically semi-autonomous sections of men's clubs. Wholly indepedent women's clubs, with their own courses and clubhouses, were rare. Within men's clubs, however, the female presence was often considerable. In the Stirling region of Scotland, for instance, it ranged from a low of one in ten of the total membership in the cases of the Milngavie and Falkirk Tryst clubs to a high of one in three at clubs like Aberfoyle and Tillicoultry. Between 1893, the date of its inception, and 1914 the number of clubs affiliated to the Ladies' Golf Union rose from 11 to 400 and their total membership from 500 to 20,000. Altogether, it has been estimated that the number of women playing golf in Britain increased from under 2,000 in the early 1890s to 40,000 by 1912, roughly 20 per cent of the entire golf-playing population. In golf, as in lawn tennis, many of these women regularly competed in inter and intra-club tournaments and mixed-sex matches were common (McCrone, 1988: 166–77; Tranter, 1989b: 37–8, 42–3; Brailsford, 1991: 140; Lowerson, 1993: 216; Birley, 1995: 100–13). The first private hockey club for adult females was formed at Molesey in 1887, the first women's hockey international

(England versus Ireland) was played in 1895 and national women's hockey associations were established for England in 1895, Wales in 1898 and Scotland in 1900. By 1911 the All-England Women's Hockey Association represented around 300 clubs, grouped into five regional and thirty-six county associations, and some 10,000 players (McCrone, 1988: 128–37; Lowerson, 1993: 213; Hargreaves, 1994: 101).

As Allen Guttmann concludes, by the outbreak of the First World War the percentage of upper- and middle-class females taking an active part in sport outside the home was significantly larger than it had been little more than a generation or so earlier (Guttmann, 1991: 117–23). Much of this increased participation in sport, moreover, involved a degree of competitiveness and physical exertion that would have been quite unacceptable to the previous generation (Parratt, 1989: 144, 146-8). Herein, perhaps, lies the reason why in the course of the late nineteenth and early twentieth centuries relatively sedate sports like croquet and archery, not so long before almost the sole options for the sporting female, increasingly failed to compete with those of a more energetic kind like hockey and lawn tennis (Park, 1989: 16).

Underlying these changes in the extent and character of elite female sport was a variety of impulses which, together, led to the emergence of attitudes more sympathetic to the participation of females in more vigorous and competitive forms of physical recreation. One of the most influential of these was the growing realisation that physical fitness was essential both to the ability of upper- and middle-class women to produce healthy babies and as a counter to the possibility that their increasing exposure to formal education would result in excessive mental strain. Reinforced by the teachings of Social Darwinism and eugenic anxieties about the cultural, political and social implications of the especially rapid decline in levels of fertility among the 'superior' social classes, adequate standards of physical fitness among upper- and middle-class females were increasingly seen as vital not only to the maintenance of the nation's efficiency but also to the prevention of the socially destabilising consequences that might follow from permitting too great an imbalance between the numbers of middle-class and working-class citizens (Atkinson, 1987: 38–41; McCrone, 1988: 195–9; 1990: 205; Holt, 1989: 117; Warren, 1993: 56; Hargreaves, 1994: 47–8, 105).

The cause of elite female sport was further buttressed by the gradual emergence of a new ideal of femininity which allowed women greater measures of independence, rationality and pleasure and which came to accept that physical fitness increased rather than decreased femininity and thus raised rather than lowered the attractiveness of women to men. In turn, through the contribution it was assumed to make to the moderation of woman's sexual desires and to the enhancement of her capacity for loyalty, rational thought, resourcefulness, determination and good humour, sport worked to train females to fit this ideal, thereby ensuring the standards of morality and behaviour that were considered essential for middle-class family life (Holt, 1989: 119; McCrone, 1990: 225; Warren, 1993: 50; Hargreaves, 1994: 89, 94, 111). In the fact that sports like archery, croquet, lawn tennis and golf provided a much-needed additional forum for social contact between the sexes many historians see yet another reason for the growing acceptance of elite female participation in sport (McCrone, 1988: 156–7; Holt, 1989: 125; Lowerson, 1989a: 205; Tranter, 1989b: 45; Reiss, 1994: 148). More controversial is the suggestion advanced by some earlier scholars that the rise of women's sport also owed much to the assistance it received from the incipent feminist movement (Atkinson, 1978; Fletcher, 1987). Subsequent scholars have been more sceptical of the suggestion that sport for women was promoted as part of the broader feminist cause (Holt, 1989: 117; Lowerson, 1989a: 205). Some, indeed, have even claimed that the rise of women's sport in late Victorian and Edwardian times owed nothing to the efforts of a feminist movement which, apart from applauding the liberating role of the bicycle, tended to view the participation of women in sport more as a distraction from than a stimulus to its attempts to improve woman's overall status in society (Park, 1989: 10, 16, 22; McCrone, 1990: 225).

In virtually the same breath as they acknowledge the advances made by upper- and middle-class females in sport, it must be emphasised that all historians of the subject are equally careful to stress the hesitant and limited nature of these advances (Mangan, 1989: 5–7; Brailsford, 1991: 140). As late as 1914, even in the elite girls' schools where it was most common, sport remained well below academic subjects and a training in social and domestic skills on the list of priorities in marked contrast to the situation in elite boys' schools; and it is far from certain that more than a minority of pupils participated in sport on a regular basis (McCrone, 1988: 85–93, 288; Warren, 1993: 57). For the bulk of middle-class girls, who did not attend an elite school and for whom school and post-school facilities for physical recreation were more restricted, the opportunities for indulging in sport were a good deal more meagre and less likely to be taken up where they did exist (McCrone, 1987: 119; Warren, 1993: 58, 60, 62). Not surprisingly, therefore, in relation to the number of women of an age and social class appropriate for admission, the number who joined curling, cycling or golf clubs remained small (Holt, 1989: 124; Tranter, 1989b: 38). The reality was that women's sport continued to be dominated by a small, atypical population of unmarried females educated in a few elite schools and colleges (Reiss, 1994: 161). For most middle-class females sport was rarely practised beyond school years and still more rarely beyond marriage (Warren, 1993, 57). Measured by the numbers and proportions that participated, women's sport was certainly more fully 'out of the closet' in 1914 than half a century earlier. But the closet door was still no more than partially open (McCrone, 1987: 119, 121).

A similar conclusion holds both for the range and type of sports available to females and for the manner in which these were practised. Even though the range of sports open to females broadened, many remained almost entirely closed to them. And even in those in which they were extensively involved segregation of the sexes was the norm and women's status strictly subordinated to that of men. Sports such as cricket, quoiting, rugby, sea-fishing and soccer excluded all but a handful of the most determined females (Holt, 1989: 128; Tranter, 1989b: 35; Williams and Woodhouse, 1991: 89; Lowerson, 1993: 48; Warren, 1993: 57). Punting was permissible but not sculling or rowing (Lowerson, 1993: 211; Warren, 1993: 57): figure-skating and equestrianism but not rhythmic gymnastics or track and field athletics (Holt, 1989: 129; Brailsford, 1991: 141; Hargreaves, 1994: 95).

Generally, women found it easier to break into sports of a more individual, gentle and less confrontational type, like golf and lawn tennis, than into team-based sports and sports requiring competitiveness, bodily contact and considerable expenditures of energy (McCrone, 1988: 154, 185; Warren, 1993: 57; Hargreaves, 1994:

51). To the majority of women as well as men the ideal of female sport remained much the same in 1914 as it had been on the eve of the late Victorian and Edwardian boom: segregated from that of men or, where integrated, always subordinate to men's control and priorities; recreational rather than combative and concerned more with the pursuit of better health, social intercourse and courtship than with honing the competitive instincts; and sufficiently restrained and ladylike in its demeanour to enhance femininity and avoid any challenge to masculinity and the functions of the male (Warren, 1993: 57; Lowerson, 1993: 208, 217–18; Hargreaves, 1994: 51, 88, 90, 109; Reiss, 1994: 147).

Far more often than not, as late as 1914, the reality closely matched the ideal. Thus, female cricketers bowled underarm not overarm in order to protect their femininity and to differentiate their game from its altogether more physical and competitive male counterpart (Warren, 1993: 57). Female archers shot with different bows, at different targets and over shorter distances than men (McCrone, 1988: 155). Public baths allocated separate times for male and female swimmers (Hargreaves, 1994: 47). Supported by the large majority of female cyclists, for whom cycling was chiefly a quest for improved health and physical attractiveness, the Cyclists' Touring Club managed to delay sponsoring competitive cycle racing for women until 1916 (Lowerson, 1993: 215; Hargreaves, 1994: 94).

To protect the masculinity of its game, the men's Hockey Association opposed the establishment of the All-England Women's Hockey Association and refused to allow it to affiliate when the AEWHA was established (Lowerson, 1993: 213; Hargreaves, 1994: 101). In the sport of golf women were expected to give way to men when playing, usually played from different tees and over nine rather than eighteen holes, were excluded from areas of the clubhouse like the bar, could neither vote nor hold office and were banned from playing at weekends or when club competitions were in progress (Lowerson, 1989a: 205; 1993, 216; Holt, 1989: 132). Even in that most mixed sex of sports, lawn tennis, every effort was made to restrict the extent of female competitiveness and responsibility. Girls were encouraged to play but never too well nor too hard and were expected always to put appearance before performance (Holt, 1989: 127–8). In spite of having more than twice as many women as men among its members, the Braid Lawn Tennis

Club of Edinburgh persistently refused to elect women to its main committees, limiting them to a separate ladies' committee responsible solely for the provision of refreshments on match days.

As the example of lawn tennis amply demonstrates, though the extent and character of elite female involvement in the public world of sport undoubtedly changed for the better during the later Victorian and Edwardian periods, continuity was at least as much a feature of women's sport as change. On the whole, bourgeois society, its females no less than its males, still preferred its women to participate in sport as spectators rather than players and as patrons and sponsors rather than as directors, shareholders and officebearers (Tranter, 1989b: 34–5, 39–40). To the extent that the active participation of women in sport was increasingly accepted it remained largely contained within a range and type of sporting activity that offered little challenge to the still broadly prevailing belief that physical recreation outside the confines of the school and the home was generally suitable only for men.

Originating in the eighteenth century and reinforced in the nineteenth century by a combination of scientific and medical orthodoxy, increasing specialisation in occupation and methods of production and the growing need for a stable family life in a rapidly changing and ever-more competitive world, the recognition of distinctive male and female biological structures led, almost inevitably, to the emergence of a social ideology which preferred to separate rather than mingle the functions of the sexes and a social practice which, by and large, succeeded in doing so. By virtue of their larger pelvises and supposedly smaller brains, greater susceptibility to ill health and psychological tendency to emotion and incoherence, passivity and cooperativeness, females were assumed to be better suited for the sphere of childrearing, domestic duties and charitable works; males, endowed with greater intelligence and muscular strength and a psychology which made them aggressive, competitive and decisive, for the sphere of public academic and political activity, gainful employment and, of course, competitive sport (Hargreaves, Jennifer, 1986: 112; 1987, 134–5, 141; 1994, 43–4; McCrone, 1987: 98, 101; 1988, 6–10, 192–4; Parratt, 1989: 142–3; Vertinsky, 1994: 149, 151, 156, 158).

Admittedly, the ideal of woman as invalid was never as prevalent as some historians have supposed. It was not merely working-class men who preferred their women to be physically fit. Even early in the Victorian period many middle-class men, too, regarded a degree of physical fitness in women as an attraction and a healthy woman as a greater asset in marriage than a perpetually unhealthy one (Guttmann, 1991: 85–6, 89–90, 96). Despite this, the belief that males and females were fashioned by anatomical differences to fulfil broadly different roles survived largely intact. Accepted as the natural order of things, this ideology resisted anything that was perceived as a threat to its persistence. The incursion of females into sport was one such threat. To some extent hostility to the participation of middle-class women in sport reflected no more than a simple desire on the part of men to create a haven free from female influence and the pressures of domestic life (Dunning, 1986: 84, 89; Lowerson, 1993: 215). In the main, however, it was driven by the widespread belief that it would undermine the ability of both men and women to perform the very different functions demanded by innate disparities in their physiologies and psychologies. To allow women to participate actively in sport, particularly in its most robust and combative forms, was to risk diminishing the capacity of sport for producing men with the kind of qualities considered essential for success in public life – courage, determination, competitiveness and perseverance. As Holt has put it, how could men be men if women were allowed to infiltrate and 'feminise' one of the key institutions through which masculinity was defined and taught? (Holt, 1989: 117; Lowerson, 1993: 205).

No less disturbing was the possibility that an involvement in sport would simultaneously undermine the capacity of women to carry out their own naturally ordained functions – to manage the household, subordinate themselves to the interests of their husbands or fathers, serve as beacons of delicacy, gentleness and moral purity in an increasingly difficult world and produce the healthy children so necessary for the future of the nation (Mangan, 1989: 2–3; Lowerson, 1993: 203, 206–7; Warren, 1993: 55; Hargreaves, 1994: 55).

Given that men too did not entirely escape the charge that an excessive commitment to sport was detrimental to their work, health and standards of behaviour, the constraints imposed on the participation of middle-class women in sport by the 'separate spheres' ideology should not be overstated (Parratt, 1989, 155). At no time during the Victorian and Edwardian eras, however, was the criticism of male sporting activity nearly so widespread or vehement as that levelled against women's sport. For every eugenist or Social Darwinist who considered sport beneficial to the health and reproductive potential of women there were many who considered its effects damaging. For every man or woman who believed that sport enhanced the attractions of the female to the male there were many who remained convinced that it masculinised women and diminished their allure. Not even those staunchest pioneers of female sport, the elite school headmistresses, intended sport as a challenge to the ideal of domesticity for women upon which the 'separate spheres' ideology insisted. In 1914 the notion that men should inhabit the public world and women the private world was still largely intact. The consequences were, first, that the extent of middle-class female participation in sport grew much more slowly than that of middle-class males and, secondly, that most of the sports which females took up were of a kind that could be slotted with reasonable comfort into the conventional image of what was considered appropriate for womanhood. By 1914 women had won themselves a more extensive place in sport than ever before, but only because they had chosen, or been permitted to choose, sports which neither allowed equal competition with men nor conflicted too dramatically with the traditional view of women as docile, fragile and subordinate. Fundamentally, sport remained a symbol and prerogative of masculinity, a reminder and reinforcer of gender differences (Clarke and Crichter, 1985: 70; McCrone, 1987: 117, 121; 1988: 13–14, 212; Hargreaves, 1994: 30, 44, 47, 51, 98–9, 108, 111). According to John Hargreaves, this is still very much the case today (Hargreaves, 1985: 225–6).

Some years ago Eric Hobsbawm suggested that the growing involvement of upper- and middle-class women in sport made a significant contribution to the wider movement for female emancipation in late Victorian and Edwardian Britain (Hobsbawm, 1983: 299). Cycling is considered by some to have played a particularly important part in beginning the process of liberating women from traditional ideological and social constraints (Rubinstein: 1977). Generally, sport historians have taken a more cautious view. By increasing social contact between the sexes, raising woman's self-confidence, self-esteem and capacity for self-determination and facilitating physical movement through the stimulus it gave to the adoption of lighter, less constricting clothing, all would accept that participation in sport contributed something to the cause of female emancipation (McCrone, 1988: 216–42, 276–9; 1990: 225; Park, 1989: 12, 18; Hargreaves, 1994: 92, 95, 109; Birley, 1995: 199). At the same time, it is broadly agreed that the contribution was modest. Few of the women who participated in sport were especially emancipated in their outlook or committed to feminist ideals, and none played a leading role in the feminist movement. Far from being revolutionaries, women golfers were not even interested in challenging the subordinate status accorded to them in the sport they played.

Cycling, that most liberating of female physical recreations, was frequently criticised by women themselves for the dangerously excessive amount of freedom it seemed to offer (Park, 1989: 10, 12, 16; Holt, 1989: 122–3; Hargreaves, 1994: 93–4; Birley, 1995: 82, 199). The pursuit of dress reform as a symbol of, and stimulus to, the cause of female emancipation was of as little interest to feminists, who regarded it with suspicion, as it was to dress reformers themselves, who were more concerned with improving women's health than their political and social standing. And, in any case, in practice the participation of women in sport had no immediate, dramatic effect on the type of clothing worn, either for sporting or other purposes. Heavy skirts, tight-lacing and figure-obscuring garments remained the predominant mode of dress for sportswomen more or less throughout the period. As exemplified by the abandonment of roller-skating for lawn tennis, for which tight-lacing was less of a hindrance, whenever there was conflict between the requirements of a game and the dictates of fashion and decorum it was invariably the former not the latter which changed (Park, 1989: 16–17, 21; Lowerson, 1993: 213). Overall, it seems, women's sport did little to lessen inequalities between the sexes. On the contrary, it may even have reinforced them (Hargreaves, 1987: 141; 1994: 109; McCrone, 1988: 13; Mangan, 1987: 5–7; Holt, 1989: 118; Lowerson, 1993: 203). Since most of the women who participated in sport were more concerned with the pursuit of better health, enjoyment or a marriage partner than with advancing their political and social status, it was unlikely to have been otherwise (Park, 1989: 10). Ultimately, the developments which occurred in the scale and character of female sport during the late nineteenth and early twentieth centuries were too limited and too conservative to do more than nibble at the fringes of established gender roles. The Victorian and Edwardian sporting 'revolution', and the immediate consequences which flowed from it, was, indeed, essentially a male phenomenon.

7

Agenda for research

Harold Perkin, echoing the view of others before him, once observed that 'the history of societies is more widely reflected in the way they spend their leisure than in their work or politics' (Perkin, 1989: 145). If intended as a serious statement of fact even the most committed student of leisure history would probably consider this an exaggeration. If intended merely as recognition and justification of the growing interest historians had for some time been showing in the evolution and significance of leisure activities it is less contentious. In the context of that aspect of leisure activity which took the form of physical recreation a disproportionate share of this interest has focused on the century or so leading up to the outbreak of the First World War, when the bases of a modern sporting culture were first effectively laid. The result is that for the nineteenth and early twentieth centuries we already have at least a broad understanding of the way in which sport – its extent, timing and organisational structure, its patterns of diffusion, its causes and consequences, its economics, the age, sex, marital and socio-occupational composition of its participants and the behaviour of its players and spectators – was transformed by the rise of urban-industrial society.

Yet, even for this period, there remain major gaps in our knowledge. If we are to achieve a more balanced appreciation of the nature of working-class sport, one of the requirements of future research must be to focus less on the new forms of codified, organised sport and more on what happened to traditional sports like dog racing, pedestrianism, pigeon-flying, quoiting, knurr and spell and long (or potshare) bowling, whose supporters were overwhelmingly working class but whose histories are still largely hidden. To resolve satisfactorily the question of what happened to levels of working-class participation in sport during Victorian and Edwardian times we require a more precise, quantitative assessment of the extent of popular sport in the preceding Georgian age than is currently available. Future research will also need to devote more attention to the sporting cultures of Scotland and Wales and the evolution of sports such as amateur athletics, badminton, billiards, bowls, cycling, darts, hockey, lawn tennis, snooker and swimming, all of which so far have been relatively neglected.

The valuable work already done on the participation of elite middle-class females in sport at school and college and on into adulthood will require to be complemented by similarly detailed work on the less well-documented experiences of aristocratic, lower-middle and, particularly, working-class females and on the attitudes of men to female involvement. Subsequent research on the behaviour of crowds at soccer matches, and other sporting events, must take greater care than has all-too-often been the case in the past to relate instances of spectator disturbance to the number of matches played and the size of crowds and, in its search for explanation, pay closer heed to the influence of environmental differences on the character of the disturbance.

Further analysis is urgently needed on chronological and spatial variations in the proportions of people who participated as players and spectators, on the age, sex, marital and social class composition of those who played, watched, administered and patronised sport, on the motives for involvement, on the precise nature of the process through which individual sports were transformed into their modern form and on the relationship which existed between individual sports in what was often a highly competitive market.

How far the extent and nature of sporting activity was affected by inter-community variations in economic and social structure and what factors determined the pace at which each sport was diffused are other questions which have yet to be adequately considered. Particular attention will have to be given to analysing the consequences of the sporting 'revolution', an aspect of the phenomenon which so far has been accorded a much lower priority than the search for causes, meanings and intentions. How much *did* sport contribute to improvements in health and a stronger sense of local and national identity? In practice, was it beneficial or detrimental to harmonious relationships between and within the different social classes? How profitable was it for the entrepreneurs and shareholders whose businesses and investments met its needs, for the workers it directly and indirectly employed and for the communities in which it was practised? Was the sport industry a cost or a benefit to the economy as a whole? To date, only the most tentative steps have been taken towards answering these questions (Mason, 1988: 139–40; Bailey, 1989: 118; Reiss, 1994: 182–4).

Most of all, perhaps, the focus of future research will need to shift away from its current preference for the best-known and prestigious institutions, promoters and performers towards a greater concern for the less famous and more obscure organisations and personalities. Much is already known about venerable bodies like the Marylebone Cricket Club, the English Football Association, the Scottish Football League and the Jockey Club and about leading clubs like Glasgow Rangers, Glasgow Celtic, West Ham United and the English first-class cricket counties, but very little about the myriad clubs and competitive structures which existed at humbler levels beneath them. Much is already known about the motives and activities of leading 'missionaries' of sport like Hely Hutchison Almond, John Guthrie Kerr and their elite public-school acolytes, but little about how far their aims and activities were shared by the considerably larger community of men, middle class as well as working class, who were equally ardent supporters of sport in their localities. Beneath the level of the grand and the famous there is a history of the more mundane and obscure still waiting to be satisfactorily uncovered. Until it is, there is a danger that our understanding of the evolution and role of sport in Victorian and Edwardian Britain will remain distorted in favour of the atypical rather than the typical. For the historian of popular culture what happened to soccer clubs like Callander Rob Roy and the Doune Vale of Teith is no less illuminating than what happened to Glasgow Rangers or Queens Park.

The agenda of questions listed above is a daunting one and is unlikely ever to be completed in full, particularly for the period before the mid-nineteenth century when direct information on sporting pastimes is rare and historians are forced to rely heavily on the scattered, impressionistic and often biased evidence contained in parliamentary and other state records, diaries, travellers' accounts, and the like. Even for the period between 1850 and

1914, when the range and depth of relevant material markedly improves, there remain serious gaps. Except for those which adopted company status, few sports clubs have left detailed records while the number of sport businesses for which evidence survives is smaller still. Even so, by careful analysis of the club and business records which do exist combined with greater use of the profusion of information on sport contained in newspapers, periodicals and specialist sporting publications and in the extant records of sports' controlling bodies, it should eventually be possible to overcome at least some of the deficiencies in our current understanding of the Victorian and Edwardian sporting world.

Bibliography

Allison, L. (1980) 'Batsman and bowler: the key relation of Victorian England', *Journal of Sport History*, 7, 5–20.

Anderson, R. D. (1987) 'Sport and the Scottish universities, 1860–1939', *International Journal of the History of Sport*, 4, 2, 177–88.

Andrews, D. (1996) 'Sport and the masculine hegemony of the modern nation: Welsh rugby, culture and society, 1890-1914', in J. Nauright and T. J. L. Chandler (eds.), *Making Men. Rugby and Masculine Identity* (London), pp. 140–57.

Arnold, A. J. (1989) 'The belated entry of professional soccer into the West Riding textile district of northern England: commercial imperatives and problems', *International Journal of the History of Sport*, 6, 3, 319–34.

Atkinson, P. (1978) 'Fitness, feminism and schooling', in S. Delamont and L. Duffin (eds.), *The Nineteenth Century Woman: Her Cultural and Physical World* (London), pp. 92–133.

—— (1987) 'The feminist physique: physical education and the medicalisation of women's education', in J. A. Mangan and R. J. Park (eds.), *From 'Fair Sex' to Feminism. Sport and the Socialization of Women in the Industrial and Post-Industrial Eras* (London), pp. 38–57.

Bailey, P. (1978) *Leisure and Class in Victorian England: Rational Recreation and the Contest for Social Control, 1830–85* (London). A pioneering study of the emergence of the middle-class ideology of 'rational' recreation and its relationship with working-class leisure activities. Based on evidence for Bolton.

—— (1989) 'Leisure, culture and the historian: reviewing the first generation of leisure historiography in Britain', *Leisure Studies*, 8, 107–27.

Bale, J. R. (1978), 'Geographical diffusion and the adoption of professionalism in football in England and Wales', *Geography*, 63, 3, 188–97.

—— (1982) *Sport and Place. A Geography of Sport in England, Scotland and Wales* (London). Analyses regional variations in the popularity of individual sports.

(1989) *Sports Geography* (London).

Birley, D. (1995) *Land of Sport and Glory. Sport and British Society, 1887–1910* (Manchester). An instructive synopsis, rich in telling detail on some of the personalities involved.

Brailsford, D. (1982) 'Sporting days in eighteenth century England', *Journal of Sport History*, 9, 3, 41–54.

   (1991) *Sport, Time and Society. The British at Play* (London). A fascinating and original study of the impact of economic modernisation on the chronology and character of sporting pastimes.

Branca, P. (1978) *Women in Europe since 1750* (London).

Chandler, T. J. L. (1988a) 'The development of a sporting tradition at Oxbridge: 1800–60', *Canadian Journal of the History of Sport*, 19, 2, 1–29.

   (1988b) 'Emergent athleticism: games in two English public schools, 1800–60', *International Journal of the History of Sport*, 5, 3, 312–30. Modifies the influence of social control motives on the initial development of organised sport in the elite public schools.

   (1991) 'Games at Oxbridge and the public schools, 1830–80: the diffusion of an innovation', *International Journal of the History of Sport*, 8, 2, 171–204.

   (1996) 'The structuring of manliness and the development of rugby football at the public schools and Oxbridge, 1830-80', in J. Nauright and T. J. L. Chandler (eds.), *Making Men. Rugby and Masculine Identity* (London), pp. 13–31.

Clarke J. and Crichter, J. (1985) *The Devil Makes Work. Leisure in Capitalist Britain* (London).

Collins, Tony (1995) 'Noa mutton, noa laaking: the origins of payment of play in rugby football, 1887-96', *International Journal of the History of Sport*, 12, 1, 33–50.

Crump, J. (1989) 'Athletics', in Mason (ed.), *Sport in Britain*, pp. 44–77.

Crump, J. and Mason, T. (1985), 'Hostile and improper demonstrations: football violence, 1880–1980', *Bulletin of the Society for the Study of Labour History*, 50, 11–12.

Cunningham, H. (1980) *Leisure in the Industrial Revolution, c. 1780–c. 1880* (London). A key text. Argues that opportunities for mass leisure increased rather than decreased in the early nineteenth century and that leisure strengthened rather than weakened social class differences.

Delves, A. (1981) 'Popular recreation and social conflict in Derby, 1800–50', in E. Yeo and S. Yeo (eds.), *Popular Culture and Class Conflict, 1560–1914* (Brighton), pp. 89–127.

Dewey, Chris. (1995) 'Socratic teachers: Part I – the opposition to the cult of athletics at Eton, 1870–1914', *International Journal of the History of Sport*, 12, 1, 51–80.

Duffin, L. (1978) 'The conspicuous consumptive: woman as an invalid', in S. Delamont and L. Duffin (eds.), *The Nineteenth Century Woman: Her Cultural and Physical World* (London), pp. 26–56.

Dunning, E. (1975) 'Industrialisation and the incipient modernisation of football', *Stadion*, 1, 103–39.

Dunning, E. and Sheard, K. (1979) *Barbarians, Gentlemen and Players. A Sociological Study of the Development of Rugby Football* (Oxford). An influential work stressing the contribution of the elite schools to the survival of folk football and its transformation into modern rugby.

Dunning, E., Murphy, P., Williams, J. and Maguire, J. (1984) 'Football hooliganism in Britain before the first world war', *International Review of the Sociology of Sport*, 9, 3/4, 214–40.

Fishwick, N. (1989) *English Football and Society, 1910-50* (Manchester).

Fletcher, S. (1987) 'The making and breaking of a female tradition: women's physical education in England, 1880-1980', in J. A. Mangan and R. J. Park (eds.), *From 'Fair Sex' to Feminism: Sport and the Socialization of Women in the Industrial and Post-Industrial Eras* (London), pp. 145–57.

Flett, K. (1989) 'Re-reading Reid: the construction of spectator sport', *International Journal of the History of Sport*, 6, 2, 256–8. With minor modifications, supports Reid.

Golby, J. M. and Purdue, A. W. (1984) *The Civilisation of the Crowd. Popular Culture in England, 1750–1900* (London).

Guttmann, A. (1969) *Sports Spectators* (New York).

   (1985) 'English sports spectators: the Restoration to the early nineteenth century', *Journal of Sport History*, 12, 2, 103–25.

   (1991) *Women's Sports: A History* (New York). From ancient Egypt to the present. Chapters 7 and 8 deal with the nineteenth century and include judicious criticism of earlier interpretations.

Halladay, E. (1987) 'Of pride and prejudice: the amateur question in English nineteenth century rowing', *International Journal of the History of Sport*, 4, 1, 39–55.

Hargreaves, Jennifer (1986) 'Where's the virtue? Where's the grace? A discussion of the social production of gender relations in and through sport', *Theory, Culture and Society*, 3, 1, 109–21.

   (1987) 'Victorian familism and the formative years of female sport', in J. A. Mangan and R. J. Park (eds.), *From 'Fair Sex' to Feminism: Sport and the Socialization of Women in the Industrial and Post-Industrial Eras* (London), pp. 130–44.

   (1994) *Sporting Females. Critical Issues in the History and Sociology of Women's Sport* (London).

Hargreaves, John (1985) 'From social democracy to authoritarian populism: state intervention in sport and physical recreation in contemporary Britain', *Leisure Studies*, 4, 219–26.

(1986a) 'The state and sport: programmed and non-programmed intervention in contemporary Britain', in L. Allison (ed.), *The Politics of Sport* (Manchester), pp. 242–61.

(1986b) *Sport, Power and Culture: A Social and Historical Analysis of Popular Sports in Britain* (New York). The most sophisticated statement of sport as an agent of social control.

Hay, J. R. (1982) 'Soccer and social control in Scotland, 1873–1978', in R. Cashman and M. McKernan (eds.), *Sport: Money, Morality and the Media* (New South Wales), pp. 223–43. Utilises quantitative data to dispute the notion of social control through sport.

Hobsbawm, E. (1983) 'Mass-producing traditions: Europe, 1870–1914', in E. Hobsbawm and T. Ranger (eds.), *The Invention of Tradition* (Cambridge), pp. 263–307.

Holt, R. J. (1988) 'Football and the urban way of life in nineteenth century Britain', in J. A. Mangan (ed.), *Pleasure, Profit and Proselytism: British Culture and Sport at Home and Abroad, 1700–1914* (London), pp. 67–85.

(1989) *Sport and the British* (Oxford). Essential reading. The most rewarding single volume on sport in modern Britain, combining stylistic elegance with an abundance of illuminating detail and perceptive analysis.

Huggins, M. (1987) 'Horse-racing on Tees-side in the nineteenth century: change and continuity', *Northern History*, 23, 98–118.

(1989) 'The spread of association football in north-east England, 1876–90: the pattern of diffusion', *International Journal of the History of Sport*, 6, 3, 299–318.

Hutchinson, J. (1975) 'Some aspects of football crowds before 1914', in Proceedings of the Conference of the Society for the Study of Labour History, *The Working Class and Leisure* (University of Sussex), pp. 7–9.

Ickringill, S. J. S. (1993) 'Amateur and professional: sport in Britain and America at the turn of the twentieth century', in J. C. Binfield and J. Stevenson (eds.), *Sport, Culture and Politics* (Sheffield), pp. 30–48.

Jarvie, G. (1991) *Highland Games: The Making of the Myth* (Edinburgh).

Korr, C. P. (1978) 'West Ham United Football Club and the beginnings of professional football in East London, 1894–1914', *Journal of Contemporary History*, 13, 2, 211–32.

Lewis, R. W. (1996) 'Football hooliganism in England before 1914: a critique of the Dunning thesis', *International Journal of the History of Sport*, 13, 3, 310–39.

Lowerson, J. (1988) 'Brothers of the angle: coarse fishing and English working-class culture, 1850-1914', in J. A. Mangan (ed.), *Pleasure, Profit and Proselytism: British Culture and Sport at Home and Abroad, 1700–1914* (London), pp. 105–27.

(1989a) 'Golf', in Mason (ed.), pp. 187–214.

(1989b) 'Angling', in Mason (ed.), pp. 12–43.

(1993) *Sport and the English Middle Classes, 1870–1914* (Manchester). An unusually wide-ranging treatment of the development of middle-class sport, especially valuable for its analysis of sport's wider economic consequences.

Maguire, J. (1986) 'Images of manliness and competing ways of living in late Victorian and Edwardian Britain', *British Journal of Sport History*, 3, 3, 265–87. Shows how the concept of manliness continued to be interpreted differently by the middle and working classes.

Malcolmson, R. W. (1973) *Popular Recreations in English Society, 1700–1850* (Cambridge). A seminal work arguing for an almost complete vacuum in working-class sport by the beginning of the Victorian period.

Mandle, W. F. (1973) 'Games people played: cricket and football in England and Victoria in the nineteenth century', *Historical Studies*, 15, 511–35.

Mangan, J. A. (1981) *Athleticism in the Victorian and Edwardian Public School: the Emergence and Consolidation of the Educational Ideology* (Cambridge). Pioneering study of the creation of the elite schools' games cult.

(1983) 'Grammar schools and the games ethic in the Victorian and Edwardian eras', *Albion*, 15, 313–35.

(1988) 'Catalyst of change: John Guthrie Kerr and the adaptation of an indigenous Scottish tradition', in J. A. Mangan (ed.), *Pleasure, Profit and Proselytism. British Culture and Sport at Home and Abroad, 1700-1914* (London), pp. 86–104.

(1989) 'The social construction of Victorian femininity: emancipation, education and exercise', *International Journal of the History of Sport*, 6, 1, 1–9.

(1996) 'Games field and battlefield: a romantic alliance in verse and the creation of militaristic masculinity', in J. Nauright and T. J. L. Chandler (eds.), *Making Men: Rugby and Masculine Identity* (London), pp. 140–57.

Mangan, J. A. (ed.) (1995) 'Tribal identities: nationalism, Europe and sport', *International Journal of the History of Sport*, Special Issue, 12, 2. Focuses on the use of sport as a force for national unity and confrontation between nations.

Martens, J. W. (1996) 'Rugby, class, amateurism and manliness: the case of rugby in northern England, 1871-95', in J. Nauright and T. J. L. Chandler (eds.), *Making Men: Rugby and Masculine Identity* (London), pp. 32–49.

Mason, Tony (1980) *Association Football and English Society, 1863–1915* (Brighton).

(1982) 'Football and the workers in England, 1880–1914', in R. Cashman and M. McKernan (eds.), *Sport: Money, Morality and the Media* (New South Wales), pp. 248–66.

(1988) 'Football and the historians', *International Journal of the History of Sport*, 5, 1, 136–40.

(1989) 'Football', in Mason (ed.), pp. 146–86.

Mason, Tony (ed.) (1989) *Sport in Britain: A Social History* (Cambridge). Informative summaries of the evolution of the major sports from their origins to the present.

McCrone, K. E. (1987) 'Play up! Play up! And play the game! Sport at the late Victorian girls' public schools', in J. A. Mangan and R. J. Park (eds.), *From 'Fair Sex' to Feminism. Sport and the Socialization of Women in the Industrial and Post-Industrial Eras* (London), pp. 97–129.

(1988) *Sport and the Physical Emancipation of English Women, 1870–1914* (London). Important, extensively researched analysis of the growing interest in sport and physical recreation among middle-class females.

(1990) 'Emancipation or recreation? The development of women's sport at the University of London', *International Journal of the History of Sport*, 7, 2, 204–29.

(1991) 'Class, gender and English women's sport c. 1890–1914', *Journal of Sport History*, 18, 1, 159–82. A rare study of working-class female involvement in sport, showing its limited extent and the hostility of middle-class females towards it.

Metcalfe, A. (1982) 'Organised sport in the mining communities of south Northumberland, 1800–99', *Victorian Studies*, 25, 4, 469–95. An important article demonstrating the independence and resilience of traditional working-class sports.

(1988) 'Football in the mining communities of east Northumberland, 1882–1914', *International Journal of the History of Sport*, 5, 3, 269–91.

(1990) 'Sport and space: a case study of the growth of recreational facilities in east Northumberland, 1850–1914', *International Journal of the History of Sport*, 7, 3, 348–64.

Moorhouse, H. F. (1987) 'Scotland against England: football and popular culture', *International Journal of the History of Sport*, 4, 2, 189–202.

Murray, Bill (1994) *Football. A History of the World Game* (Aldershot).

Myerscough, J. (1974) 'The recent history of the use of leisure time', in I. Appleton (ed.), *Leisure Research and Policy* (Edinburgh), pp. 1–16.

Orr, W. (1982) *Deer Forests, Landlords and Crofters: the Western Highlands in Victorian and Edwardian Times* (Edinburgh).

Park, J. (1989) 'Sport, dress reform and the emancipation of women in Victorian England: a reappraisal', *International Journal of the History of Sport*, 6, 1, 10–30. Suggests that there was little connection between female sport and feminism.

Parratt, C. M. (1989) 'Athletic womanhood: explaining sources for female sport in Victorian and Edwardian England', *Journal of Sport History*, 16, 2, 140–57.

Perkin, H. (1989) 'Teaching the nations how to play: sport and society in the British Empire and Commonwealth', *International Journal of the History of Sport*, 6, 2, 145–55.

Reid, D. A. (1988) 'Folk football, the aristocracy and cultural change: a critique of Dunning and Sheard', *International Journal of the History of Sport*, 5, 2, 224–38. Criticises the argument that the decline of folk football was due chiefly to the withdrawal of aristocratic patronage.

Reiss, Steven A. (1994) 'From pitch to putt: sport and class in Anglo-American sport', *Journal of Sport History*, 21, 2, 138–83. A summary and critique of the perceived role of class in sport, with suggestions for the future direction of research.

Rubinstein, D. (1977) 'Cycling in the 1890s', *Victorian Studies*, 21, 1, 47–71.

Russell, D. (1988) 'Sporadic and curious: the emergence of rugby and soccer zones in Yorkshire and Lancashire, c.1860-1914', *International Journal of the History of Sport*, 5, 2, 185–205.

Sandiford, K. A. P. (1994) *Cricket and the Victorians* (Aldershot). An intriguing analysis of the broader significance of cricket for Victorian society.

Sandiford, K. A. P. and Vamplew, W. (1986) 'The peculiar economics of English cricket before 1914', *British Journal of Sport History*, 3, 3, 311–26.

Shipley, S. (1989) 'Boxing', in Mason (ed.), pp. 78–115.

Speak, N. A. (1988) 'Social stratification and participation in sport in mid-Victorian England with particular reference to Lancaster, 1840–70', in J. A. Mangan (ed.), *Pleasure, Profit and Proselytism: British Culture and Sport at Home and Abroad, 1700–1914* (London), pp. 42–66.

Thompson, F. M. L. (1981) 'Social control in Victorian Britain', *Economic History Review*, 34, 2, 189–208. A powerful criticism of the influence of social control imperatives on the evolution of working-class behaviour and culture.

Tischler, S. (1981) *Footballers and Businessmen: the Origins of Professional Soccer in England* (London).

Tranter, N. (1987a) 'Popular sports and the Industrial Revolution in Scotland: the evidence of the Statistical Accounts', *International Journal of the History of Sport*, 4, 1, 21–38. Suggests no serious decline in popular sport between the late eighteenth and mid-nineteenth centuries. Compare with Cunningham and Malcolmson.

(1987b) 'The social and occupational structure of organised sport in central Scotland during the nineteenth century', *International Journal of the History of Sport*, 4, 3, 301–14. Based on census enumerator and newspaper data.

(1989a) 'The patronage of organised sport in central Scotland, 1820–1900', *Journal of Sport History*, 16, 3, 227–47.

(1989b) 'Organised sport and the middle-class woman in nineteenth century Scotland', *International Journal of the History of Sport*, 6, 1, 31–48.

(1990a) 'Organised sport and the working classes of central Scotland, 1820-1900: the neglected sport of quoiting', in R. J. Holt (ed.), *Sport and the Working Class in Modern Britain* (Manchester), pp. 45–66.

(1990b) 'The chronology of organised sport in nineteenth century Scotland: a regional study. Patterns', *International Journal of the History of Sport*, 7, 2, 188–203.

(1990c) 'The chronology of organised sport in nineteenth century Scotland: a regional study. II. Causes', *International Journal of the History of Sport*, 7, 3, 365–87.

(1993) 'The first football club?', *International Journal of the History of Sport*, 10, 1, 104–7.

(1995) 'The Cappielow riot and the composition and behaviour of soccer crowds in late Victorian Scotland', *International Journal of the History of Sport*, 12, 3, 125–40.

Vamplew, W. (1976) *The Turf: a Social and Economic History of Horse Racing* (London).

(1980) 'Sports crowd disorder in Britain, 1870–1914: causes and controls', *Journal of Sport History*, 7, 1, 5–20.

(1982) 'The economics of a sports industry: Scottish gate-money football, 1890–1914', *Economic History Review*, 35, 4, 549–67.

(1988a) 'Sport and industrialisation: an economic interpretation of the change in popular sport in nineteenth century England', in J. A. Mangan (ed.), *Pleasure, Profit and Proselytism. British Culture and Sport at Home and Abroad, 1700-1914* (London), pp. 7–20.

(1988b) *Pay Up and Play the Game. Professional Sport in Britain, 1875–1914* (Cambridge). The first systematic study of the economics of some of the principal spectator sports of late Victorian and Edwardian Britain.

(1989) 'Horse-racing', in Mason (ed.), pp. 215–44.

Vertinsky, P. (1994) 'The social construction of the gendered body: exercise and the exercise of power', *Journal of Sport History*, 11, 147–71.

Walvin, J. (1978) *Leisure and Society, 1830–1950* (London). Despite its age, still a useful summary of the characteristics and causes of the rise of modern sport in England.

Warren, A. (1993) 'Sport, youth and gender in Britain, 1880–1940', in J. C. Binfield and J. Stevenson (eds.), *Sport, Culture and Politics* (Sheffield), pp. 48–71.

Wigglesworth, N. (1986) 'A history of rowing in the north-west of England', *British Journal of Sport History*, 3, 2, 145–57.

Williams, G. (1988) 'From popular culture to public cliche: image and identity in Wales, 1890-1914', in J. A. Mangan (ed.), *Pleasure, Profit and Proselytism. British Culture and Sport at Home and Abroad, 1700–1914* (London), pp. 128–43.

(1989) 'Rugby union', in Mason (ed.), pp. 308–43.

Williams, J. (1989) 'Cricket', in Mason (ed.), pp. 116–45.

Williams, J. and Woodhouse, J. (1991) 'Can play, will play? Women and football in Britain', in J. Williams and S. Wagg (eds.), *British Football and Social Change: Getting into Europe* (Leicester), pp. 85–108.

Index

All England Croquet Association, 16
All England Croquet Club, 22
All England Women's Hockey Association, 88; number of clubs, 85; number of players, 85
Allan Glen's school, 67
Almond, Hely Hutchison, 96
Amateur Athletic Club, 42
Amateur Athletics Association, 26, 42; attitude to commercialism and professionalism, 42; formation, 24; number of clubs, 23
Amateur Boxing Association, 24
angling, 15–16, 18–19, 34, 39–40, 67, 76; attractions of, 53, 59–60, 64; females in, 79, 87; national associations, 24; number of clubs, 23, 24; number of participants, 16, 23
animal blood sports, 5–6, 10–11; females in, 78
Archer, Fred, 67
archery, 18, 40; females in, 81–2, 85–86, 88
athletics, 17, 40, 54, 95; attractions of, 64; females in, 78–9, 81–2, 87; number of meetings, 24

badger baiting, 5–6
badminton, 16, 22, 28, 39, 95; females in, 81, 83
Badminton Association: formation, 24; number of clubs, 23, 83
Bale, John, 30
Barclay, Captain, 6
basketball: females in, 81
battledore and shuttlecock, 83; females in, 81
bear baiting, 6
billiards, 95
Blackwood, Alexander, 57
boatracing, see rowing
bowling, 16, 17, 28, 95; attractions of, 57, 59–61, 64; club subscriptions, 42; clubs, 42, 52, 54, 82; females in, 82; indoor, 60; long or potshare, 6, 94; number of participants, 16
Bowling Association, England, formation, 24; number of clubs, 23–4; Scotland, formation, 25; Wales, formation, 25
boxing, 1, 16–17, 19, 22, 27, 29, 32, 33–4, 36; attractions of, 59–60
Boyne, Lord, 71
Bradshaw, Joseph, 67
Braid Lawn Tennis Club, 88–9

New Studies in Economic and Social History

Previously published as

Studies in Economic and Social History

Titles in the series available from the Macmillan Press Limited

Economic History Society

The Economic History Society, which numbers around 3000 members, publishes the Economic History Review four times a year (free to members) and holds an annual conference.

Enquiries about membership should be addressed to

The Assistant Secretary
Economic History Society
P O Box 70
Kingswood
Bristol
BS15 5TB

Full-time students may join at special rates.